CAMBRIDGE LIBRARY COLLECTION

Books of enduring scholarly value

Travel and Exploration

The history of travel writing dates back to the Bible, Caesar, the Vikings and the Crusaders, and its many themes include war, trade, science and recreation. Explorers from Columbus to Cook charted lands not previously visited by Western travellers, and were followed by merchants, missionaries, and colonists, who wrote accounts of their experiences. The development of steam power in the nineteenth century provided opportunities for increasing numbers of 'ordinary' people to travel further, more economically, and more safely, and resulted in great enthusiasm for travel writing among the reading public. Works included in this series range from first-hand descriptions of previously unrecorded places, to literary accounts of the strange habits of foreigners, to examples of the burgeoning numbers of guidebooks produced to satisfy the needs of a new kind of traveller - the tourist.

A Short Narrative of the Second Voyage of the Prince Albert, in Search of Sir John Franklin

William Kennedy (1814–1890) was an explorer and fur trader. In 1851 he was recommended to Lady Franklin as the commander of her second sponsored expedition in search of her husband, Arctic explorer Sir John Franklin (1786–1847), who had not returned from his 1845 expedition to chart the remaining unexplored section of the Arctic and the Northwest Passage. This volume first published in 1853 contains Kennedy's account of his 1851 Arctic expedition to rescue Sir John Franklin. Written in the form of a diary, Kennedy describes in detail the hazardous conditions of the Arctic. The crew's experiences including snow blindness, frostbite, scurvy and explorations of land on foot accompanied by Husky dogs are described in detail. Kennedy's use of Inuit survival methods and the type of provisions which were used are also described, providing valuable insights into early nineteenth century methods of Arctic exploration.

T0372746

Cambridge University Press has long been a pioneer in the reissuing of out-of-print titles from its own backlist, producing digital reprints of books that are still sought after by scholars and students but could not be reprinted economically using traditional technology. The Cambridge Library Collection extends this activity to a wider range of books which are still of importance to researchers and professionals, either for the source material they contain, or as landmarks in the history of their academic discipline.

Drawing from the world-renowned collections in the Cambridge University Library, and guided by the advice of experts in each subject area, Cambridge University Press is using state-of-the-art scanning machines in its own Printing House to capture the content of each book selected for inclusion. The files are processed to give a consistently clear, crisp image, and the books finished to the high quality standard for which the Press is recognised around the world. The latest print-on-demand technology ensures that the books will remain available indefinitely, and that orders for single or multiple copies can quickly be supplied.

The Cambridge Library Collection will bring back to life books of enduring scholarly value (including out-of-copyright works originally issued by other publishers) across a wide range of disciplines in the humanities and social sciences and in science and technology.

A Short Narrative of the Second Voyage of the Prince Albert, in Search of Sir John Franklin

WILLIAM KENNEDY

CAMBRIDGE
UNIVERSITY PRESS

CAMBRIDGE UNIVERSITY PRESS

Cambridge, New York, Melbourne, Madrid, Cape Town, Singapore,
São Paolo, Delhi, Dubai, Tokyo

Published in the United States of America by Cambridge University Press, New York

www.cambridge.org
Information on this title: www.cambridge.org/9781108019651

© in this compilation Cambridge University Press 2010

This edition first published 1853
This digitally printed version 2010

ISBN 978-1-108-01965-1 Paperback

SOMERSET HOUSE

MIDWINTER VISIT TO FURY ISLAND.

J COVENTRY, LITH

A SHORT NARRATIVE

OF THE

SECOND VOYAGE

OF

THE PRINCE ALBERT,

IN

SEARCH OF SIR JOHN FRANKLIN.

BY

WILLIAM KENNEDY,

COMMANDING THE EXPEDITION.

WITH ILLUSTRATIONS, AND A MAP BY ARROWSMITH.

LONDON:

W. H. DALTON, COCKSPUR STREET.

1853.

TO

LADY FRANKLIN,

UNDER WHOSE AUSPICES AND DIRECTION THE

EXPEDITION TO PRINCE REGENT'S INLET

IN

SEARCH OF SIR JOHN FRANKLIN AND HIS COMPANIONS

WAS UNDERTAKEN,

AND TO THE SUBSCRIBERS WHO AIDED HER,

This Narrative of the Voyage

IS RESPECTFULLY INSCRIBED

BY THEIR OBEDIENT SERVANT,

WILLIAM KENNEDY.

PREFACE.

THE following little work contains a narrative of
the last Voyage of the Prince Albert to the Arctic
Seas in search of Sir John Franklin; a chart of
the geographical discoveries effected in the course of
it; and an appendix, embracing a few Nautical and
Meteorological details.

Although in placing before the public, the zealous
and indefatigable labours of those by whom I was
accompanied on the voyage, I feel that I am but
doing them justice, I have had another motive in
committing these pages to the press, in the desire to
assist,—as far as my experience warrants my expressing
an opinion on the subject,—in disabusing the public
mind of many unfounded and frivolous apprehensions tending to bring into discredit any further
attempts to prosecute the search for our missing
countrymen. I am glad to think that such apprehensions are already giving way to wiser and juster
views of our policy and our duty in this respect.

I can testify, at least, to the very great interest everywhere felt in the question, both in England and America, among those with whom circumstances have brought me into communication; and I should be unpardonable were I to neglect to record here my deep sense of the many obligations, and the many esteemed personal friends for which I am indebted solely to my fortuitous connexion with an Expedition in search of Sir John Franklin.

The original offer of my services to Lady Franklin was made from Canada, and my appointment to the "Prince Albert" no sooner became known, than I was supplied, through the public-spirited exertions of Mr. Fisher, the Mayor of Hamilton, in that Province, with a free conveyance by the American Railroad Company from Buffalo to New York. Here I had the privilege of making the acquaintance of the noble-minded and munificent Mr. Grinnell, through whose interest I was furnished with a free passage to England in one of Cunard's steamers. I cannot but regard it as a most fortunate circumstance that one of my fellow-passengers in this voyage was Sir Edward Belcher. I need not dwell upon the interest which

this distinguished officer, and warm friend of Arctic
search, manifested in the object of my mission; but
I should indeed be forgetful, as well as ungrateful,
were I to pass over without acknowledgment, the
frank courtesy and the generous and unwearied kindness I experienced from him during the period I had
the happiness of enjoying his acquaintance. Through
his interest with the Railroad Directors of the Liverpool and London lines, my way was literally franked
through the length and breadth of the land. From
Liverpool* to London, from London to Hull, from
Hull to Aberdeen, and thence to the Orkneys, I had
simply to present Sir Edward Belcher's letter of intro-
duction at the various offices of the Railroad and Steam
Navigation Companies, and a free passage was at once
accorded to me. And this interest in the humane and
benevolent mission in which I had the privilege of
being engaged was not confined to public bodies.

I have had occasion, in the course of the narrative,

* The proprietor of the Adelphi Hotel in Liverpool, on learning my
name and object, declined, in the handsomest manner, to accept any
settlement of the somewhat heavy bill, which a residence in a first-
class house in the Capital of the West, ordinarily entails upon the
traveller.

to acknowledge many proofs of the interest felt in
the general objects of our Expedition by individuals
in various parts of England. To Mr. Barrow, of the
Admiralty, whose name is so intimately associated
with the efforts which have been made for the rescue
of our absent countrymen, and on whose shoulders
the mantle of his father has indeed descended, my
thanks are particularly due, for his constant and unremitting kindness and thoughtful care for whatever
could add to our comfort or ensure the success of
our undertaking. To my old and valued friend, Mr.
Harding, of Islington, my thanks are no less due,
for his most useful contributions to the outfit of our
winter travelling parties, and for his sound and
judicious suggestions in the organization of our land
journeys, which his unrivalled local experience, acquired during a residence of twenty years in the
northern part of Hudson's Bay, rendered truly
valuable.

To the noble-minded Lady, under whose auspices
the Expedition was equipped—did not I know how
distasteful public acknowledgments on such a subject
or publicity of any kind are to her—I would fain ex-

press my obligations for innumerable acts of personal kindness received at her hands; and my admiration of that unwearied and unexampled devotion with which she has sacrificed her health, her strength, and all her worldly means, to the search for her distinguished husband, and her gallant friends and countrymen.

Were I, however, to record all in the way of obligation, which ought to be recorded, I fear that my preface would prove nearly as big as my book. Let me, therefore, by this general acknowledgment, assure each and all of our numerous friends, that if every act of kindness and of sympathy for the cause on which we were engaged has not always been mentioned, it has assuredly not been forgotten either by me or by any one connected with the Expedition in the Prince Albert.

East Islington Institution,
December, 1852.

CONTENTS.

INTRODUCTION.

CHAPTER I.

FROM ABERDEEN TO CAPE FAREWELL.

CHAPTER II.

FROM CAPE FAREWELL TO PORT LEOPOLD.

CHAPTER III.

FROM PORT LEOPOLD TO WINTER QUARTERS IN BATTY BAY, PRINCE REGENT'S INLET.

CHAPTER IV.

WINTER JOURNEY TO FURY BEACH.

CHAPTER V.

THE LONG JOURNEY.

CHAPTER VI.

HOMEWARD BOUND.

APPENDIX.

LIST OF PLATES.

SECOND VOYAGE

OF

THE PRINCE ALBERT.

INTRODUCTION.

VARIETY OF OPINIONS AS TO THE DIRECTION TAKEN
BY SIR JOHN FRANKLIN'S EXPEDITION——GENERAL
WANT OF ACCURATE INFORMATION AS TO FRANKLIN'S
INSTRUCTIONS——THE ADMIRALTY INSTRUCTIONS TO
THE EREBUS AND TERROR IN *EXTENSO*——LAST
LETTERS FROM SIR JOHN FRANKLIN, CAPT. FITZ-
JAMES, AND MRS. BLENKY —— THE EREBUS AND
TERROR LAST SEEN BY CAPT. MARTIN AND CAPT.
DANNETT OF THE WHALER " PRINCE OF WALES "
——FIRST INTELLIGENCE OF TRACES OF THE MISSING
SHIPS AT CAPE RILEY BROUGHT HOME BY THE
" PRINCE ALBERT."

IT is perhaps a natural result of the various Expeditions which have left this country within the last

few years, in search of Sir John Franklin, that,
amidst the universal interest excited in the fate of
the missing vessels, the circumstances under which
Franklin's own Expedition left England, now upwards of six years ago, have been in some degree lost
sight of. Nothing is more common in conversation,
and in the statements of the daily press, and even in
publications of higher pretensions, than to find plans
and proposals brought forward for the relief of our
absent countrymen—professedly based upon what
are believed to have been Franklin's instructions,
but which turn out, upon inquiry, to have formed
no part either of his instructions, or of his intentions.

Under such circumstances, I have felt that I cannot better introduce the following narrative of one of
the latest attempts which have been made to penetrate the mystery which still unfortunately envelops
the fate of the Erebus and Terror, than by placing
before my reader the instructions issued to the
Expedition, on its leaving England in the spring
of 1845, of which the following is an authentic
copy.

Copy of Instructions to Captain Sir John Franklin, K.C.H.,
Her Majesty's Ship Erebus, dated 5th May, 1845.
By the Commissioners for executing the office of Lord
High Admiral of the United Kingdom of Great
Britain and Ireland.

1. Her Majesty's Government having deemed it expedient that a further attempt should be made for the accomplishment of a north-west passage by sea from the Atlantic to the Pacific Ocean, of which passage a small portion only remains to be completed, we have thought proper to appoint you to the command of the expedition to be fitted out for that service, consisting of Her Majesty's Ships " Erebus " and " Terror;" and you are hereby required and directed, so soon as the said ships shall be in all respects ready for sea, to proceed forthwith in the " Erebus" under your command, taking with you Her Majesty's ship " Terror," her captain (Crozier) having been placed by us under your orders, taking also with you the " Barretto Junior," transport, which has been directed to be put at your disposal for the purpose of carrying out portions of your provisions, clothing, and other stores.

2. On putting to sea, you are to proceed, in the first place, by such a route as, from the wind and weather, you

may deem to be the most suitable for dispatch, to Davis' Strait, taking the transport with you to such a distance up that Strait as you may be able to proceed without impediment from ice, being careful not to risk that vessel by allowing her to be set in the ice, or exposed to any violent contact with it ; you will then avail yourself of the earliest opportunity of clearing the transport of the provisions and stores with which she is charged for the use of the expedition, and you are then to send her back to England, giving to the agent or master such directions for his guidance as may appear to you most proper, and reporting by that opportunity your proceedings to our secretary for our information.

3. You will then proceed in the execution of your orders into Baffin's Bay, and get as soon as possible to the western side of the Strait, provided it should appear to you that the ice chiefly prevails on the eastern side or near the middle, the object being to enter Lancaster Sound with as little delay as possible ; but as no specific directions can be given, owing to the position of the ice varying from year to year, you will, of course, be guided by your own observations as to the course most eligible to be taken, in order to ensure a speedy arrival in the Sound above mentioned.

4. As, however, we have thought fit to cause each ship to be fitted with a small steam-engine and propeller, to be used only in pushing the ships through channels between masses of ice, when the wind is adverse or in a calm, we trust the difficulty usually found in such cases will be much obviated, but as the supply of fuel to be taken in the ships is necessarily small, you will use it only in cases of difficulty.

5. Lancaster Sound, and its continuation through Barrow Strait, having been four times navigated without any impediment by Sir Edward Parry, and since frequently by whaling ships, will probably be found without any obstacles from ice or islands; and Sir Edward Parry having also proceeded from the latter in a straight course to Melville Island, and returned without experiencing any, or very little difficulty, it is hoped that the remaining portion of the passage, about 900 miles, to Bhering's Strait may also be found equally free from obstruction; and in proceeding to the westward, therefore, you will not stop to examine any openings either to the northward or southward in that Strait, but continue to push to the westward without loss of time in the latitude of about $74\frac{1}{4}°$, till you have reached the longitude of that portion of land on which Cape Walker is situated, or about 98°

west. From that point we desire that every effort be used to endeavour to penetrate to the southward and westward, in a course as direct towards Bhering's Strait as the position and extent of the ice, or the existence of land, at present unknown, may admit.

6. We direct you to this particular part of the Polar Sea as affording the best prospect of accomplishing the passage to the Pacific, in consequence of the unusual magnitude and apparently fixed state of the barrier of ice observed by the "Hecla" and "Griper," in the year 1820 off Cape Dundas, the south-western extremity of Melville Island; and we, therefore, consider that loss of time would be incurred in renewing the attempt in that direction; but should your progress in the direction before ordered be arrested by ice of a permanent appearance, and that when passing the mouth of the Strait between Devon and Cornwallis's Islands, you had observed that it was open and clear of ice, we desire that you will duly consider, with reference to the time already consumed, as well as to the symptoms of a late or early close of the season, whether that channel might not offer a more practicable outlet from the Archipelago, and a more ready access to the open sea, where there would be neither islands nor banks to arrest and fix the floating masses of

ice, and if you should have advanced too far to the south-westward to render it expedient to adopt this new course before the end of the present season, and if, therefore, you should have determined to winter in that neighbour-hood, it will be a matter for your mature deliberation, whether in the ensuing season you would proceed by the above-mentioned Strait, or whether you would persevere to the south-westward, according to the former directions.

7. You are well aware, having yourself been one of the intelligent travellers who have traversed the American shore of the Polar Sea, that the groups of islands that stretch from that shore to the northward to a distance not yet known do not extend to the westward further than about the 120th degree of western longitude, and that beyond this, and to Bhering's Strait no land is visible from the American shore of the Polar Sea.

8. Should you be so fortunate as to accomplish a passage through Bhering's Strait, you are then to proceed to the Sandwich Islands, to refit the ships and refresh the crews, and if during your stay at such place, a safe opportunity should occur of sending one of your officers or despatches to England by Panama, you are to avail yourself of such opportunity to forward to us as full a detail of your pro-ceedings and discoveries as the nature of the conveyance

may admit of, and in the event of no such opportunity offering during your stay at the Sandwich Islands, you are on
quitting them to proceed with the two ships under your
command off Panama, there to land an officer with such
despatches, directing him to make the best of his way to
England with them, in such a manner as our Consul at
Panama shall advise, after which you are to lose no time
in returning to England by way of Cape Horn.

9. If at any period of your voyage the season shall
be so far advanced as to make it unsafe to navigate the
ships, and the health of your crews, the state of the ships
and all concurrent circumstances should combine to induce you to form the resolution of wintering in those
regions you are to use your best endeavours to discover
a sheltered and safe harbour, where the ships may be
placed in security for the winter, taking such measures
for the health and comfort of the people committed to
your charge as the materials with which you are provided
for housing in the ships may enable you to do—and if
you should find it expedient to resort to this measure,
and you should meet with any inhabitants, either Esquimaux or Indians, near the place where you winter, you
are to endeavour by every means in your power to cul-
tivate a friendship with them, by making them presents

of such articles as you may be supplied with, and which
may be useful or agreeable to them ; you will, however,
take care not to suffer yourself to be surprised by them,
but use every precaution, and be constantly on your
guard against any hostility ; you will, by offering rewards
to be paid in such manner as you may think best, pre-
vail on them to carry to any of the settlements of the
Hudson's Bay Company, an account of your situation
and proceedings, with an urgent request that it may
be forwarded to England with the utmost possible
dispatch.

10. In an undertaking of this description, much must
be always left to the discretion of the commanding officer,
and as the objects of this Expedition have been fully
explained to you, and you have already had much
experience on service of this nature, we are convinced
we cannot do better than leave it to your judgment in
the event of your not making a passage this season,
either to winter on the coast with the view of following
up next season any hopes or expectations which your
observations this year may lead you to entertain, or to
return to England to report to us the result of such
observations, always recollecting our anxiety for the
health, comfort and safety, of yourself, your officers and

men; and you will duly weigh how far the advantages of starting next season from an advanced position may be counterbalanced by what may be suffered during the winter, and by the want of such refreshment and refitting as would be afforded by your return to England.

11. We deem it right to caution you against suffering the two vessels placed under your orders to separate, except in the event of accident or unavoidable necessity; and we desire you to keep up the most unreserved communications with the commander of the "Terror," placing in him every proper confidence, and acquainting him with the general tenor of your orders, and with your views and intentions from time to time in the execution of them, that the service may have the full benefit of your united efforts in the prosecution of such a service; and that in the event of unavoidable separation, or of any accident to yourself, Captain Crozier may have the advantage of knowing up to the latest practicable period all your ideas and intentions relative to a satisfactory completion of this interesting undertaking.

12. We also recommend, that as frequent an exchange take place as conveniently may be of the observations made in the two ships; that any scientific discovery made by the one, be as quickly as possible communicated

for the advantage and guidance of the other, in making
their future observations, and to increase the probability
of the observations of both being preserved.

13. We have caused a great variety of valuable instruments to be put on board the ships under your orders, of
which you will be furnished with a list, and for the
return of which you will be held responsible; among
these are instruments of the latest improvements for
making a series of observations on terrestrial magnetism,
which are at this time peculiarly desirable and strongly
recommended by the President and Council of the Royal
Society, that the important advantage be derived from
observations taken in the North Polar Sea, in co-operation
with the observers who are at present carrying on an
uniform system at the magnetic observatories established
by England in her distant territories, and through her
influence in other parts of the world; and the more
desirable is this co-operation in the present year, when
these splendid establishments which do so much honour
to the nations who have cheerfully erected them at a
great expense, are to cease. The only magnetical
observations that have been obtained very partially in
the Arctic Regions are now a quarter of a century old,
and it is known that the phenomena are subject to

considerable secular changes. It is also stated by
Colonel Sabine that the instruments and methods of
observation have been so greatly improved that the earlier
observations are not to be named in point of precision
with those which would now be made ; and he concludes
by observing that the passage through the Polar Sea
would afford the most important service that now
remains to be performed towards the completion of the
magnetic survey of the globe.

14. Impressed with the importance of this subject we
have deemed it proper to request Lieut.-Colonel Sabine
to allow Commander Fitzjames to profit by his valuable
instructions, and we direct you therefore to place this
important branch of science under the immediate charge
of Commander Fitzjames ; and as several other officers
have also received similar instructions at Woolwich you
will therefore cause observations to be made daily on
board each of the ships whilst at sea (and when not
prevented by weather and other circumstances), on the
magnetic variation, dip and intensity, noting at the time
the temperature of the air, and of the sea at the surface
and at different depths ; and you will be careful that in
harbour and on other favourable occasions those observations shall be attended to, by means of which the influence

of the ship's iron on the result obtained at sea may be computed and allowed for.

15. In the possible event of the ships being detained during a winter in the high latitudes, the Expedition has been supplied with a portable observatory, and with instruments similar to those which are employed in the fixed magnetical and meteorological observatories instituted by Her Majesty's Government in several of the British colonies.

16. It is our desire that in case of such detention observations should be made with these instruments according to the system adopted in the aforesaid observatories, and detailed directions will be supplied for this purpose, which with the instructions received at Woolwich, will be found, as we confidently anticipate, to afford full and sufficient guidance for such observations, which will derive from their locality peculiar interest and a high theoretical value.

17. We have also directed instruments to be especially provided for observations on atmospherical refraction at very low altitudes, in case of the Expedition being detained during a winter in the high latitudes ; on this subject also particular directions will be supplied, and you will add any other meteorological observations that may occur to you of general utility ; you will also take occasion, to

try the depth of the sea and nature of the bottom, the rise, direction and strength of the tides, and the set and velocity of currents.

18. And you are to understand that although the effecting a passage from the Atlantic to the Pacific is the main object of this expedition, yet that the ascertaining the true geographical position of the different points of land near which you may pass, so far as can be effected without detention of the ships in their progress westward, as well as such other observations as you may have opportunities of making in natural history, geography, &c. in parts of the globe either wholly unknown or little visited, must prove most valuable and interesting to the science of our country ; and we therefore desire you to give your unremitting attention, and to call that of all the officers under your command to these points, as being objects of high interest and importance.

19. For the purpose not only of ascertaining the set of the currents in the Arctic seas, but also of affording more frequent chances of hearing of your progress, we desire that you do frequently after you have passed the latitude 65° north, and once every day when you shall be in an ascertained current, throw overboard a bottle or copper cylinder closely sealed, and containing a paper stating the date and position at which it is launched, and you

will give similar orders to the commander of the "Terror,"
to be executed in case of separation, on which is printed
in several languages, a request, that whoever may find
it should take measures for transmitting it to this office.

20. You are to make use of every means in your power
to collect and preserve specimens of the animal, mineral,
and vegetable kingdoms, should circumstances place such
within your reach without causing your detention ; and
of the larger animals, you are to cause accurate drawings
to be made to accompany and elucidate the descriptions
of them.   In this, as well as in every other part of your
scientific duty, we trust that you will receive material
assistance from the officers under your command, several
of whom are represented to us as well-qualified in these
respects.

21. In the event of any irreparable accident happening
to either of the two ships, you are to cause the officers
and crew of the disabled ship to be removed into the
other, and with her singly, to proceed in prosecution of
the voyage, or return to England, according as circumstances shall appear to require, understanding that the
officers and crews of both ships are hereby authorised
and required to continue to perform the duties, according
to their respective ranks and stations, on board either
ship to which they may be so removed in the event of an

occurrence of this nature. Should unfortunately your
own ship be the one disabled, you are in that case to take
the command of the " Terror ;" and in the event of any
fatal accident happening to yourself, Captain Crozier is
hereby authorized to take the command of the " Erebus,"
placing the officer of the Expedition who may then be
next in seniority to him in command of the " Terror."
Also in the event of your own inability by sickness, or
otherwise, at any period of this service, to continue to
carry these instructions into execution, you are to
transfer them to the officer the next in command to you
employed on the Expedition, who is hereby required to
execute them in the best manner he can for the attainment of the several objects herein set forth.

22. You are, while executing the service pointed out
in these instructions, to take every opportunity that may
offer of acquainting our secretary for our information
with your progress, and on your arrival in England, you
are immediately to repair to this office, in order to lay
before us a full account of your proceedings in the whole
course of your voyage ; taking care before you leave the
ship to demand from the officers, petty officers, and all
other persons on board, the logs and journals they may
have kept ; together with any drawings or charts they
may have made, which are all to be sealed up ; and you

will issue similar directions to Captain Crozier and his officers. The said logs, journals, or other documents to be thereafter disposed of as we may think proper to determine.

23. In the event of England becoming involved in hostilities with any other power during your absence, you are nevertheless clearly to understand that you are not on any account to commit any hostile act whatsoever; the expedition under your orders being only intended for the purpose of discovery and science, and it being the practice of all civilized nations to consider vessels so employed as excluded from the operations of war: and confiding in this feeling, we should trust that you would receive every assistance from the ships or subjects of any foreign power which you may fall in with; but special application to that effect has been made to the respective Governments.

Given under our hands this 5th day of May, 1845.

(Signed)   HADDINGTON.

G. COCKBURN.

W. H. GAGE.

SIR JOHN FRANKLIN, K.C.H.
Captain of H.M.S. " Erebus," at Woolwich.

By command of their Lordships,

(Signed)   W. A. B. HAMILTON.

c

The latest communication received from Franklin, subsequent to his departure from England, is dated 11th July, 1845, from Whale Fish Islands, and is addressed to his old friend Colonel Sabine.

After stating that the Erebus and Terror had on board provisions and stores for three years, complete from that date, *i.e.* up to July, 1848, he continues— "I hope my dear wife and daughter will not be over anxious if we should not return by the time they have fixed upon; and I must beg of you to give them the benefit of your advice and experience when that arrives; for you know well that even after the second winter, without success in our object, we should wish to try some other channel, if the state of our provisions and the health of the crews justify it."

On the following day (12th July,) Captain Fitz-james wrote to his friend Mr. Barrow—"We shall start with three years provisions *and the engine!* We hear that this is supposed to be a clear season, but however, clear or not clear, we must go ahead, as the Yankees have it, and if we don't get through it won't be our fault."

The Erebus was spoken on the 22nd of the same

month by Captain Martin of the Enterprise, in lat. 75o 10' N., and long. 66o W. The information of Captain Martin, as communicated in the following letter to the "Times" newspaper, by Captain Penny, is important, not only as containing the evidence of the person who last spoke the Erebus, but also from the cheering assurance it affords us of the providence and foresight evinced by Franklin while yet on the very threshold of his enterprise :—

Aberdeen, Dec. 20, 1851.

TO THE EDITOR OF THE TIMES.

SIR,—I have lately been at Peterhead (my native place), and have learnt a very important fact from my old acquaintance Captain Martin, who, when commanding the whaler Enterprise in 1845, was the last person to communicate with Sir John Franklin.

The Enterprise was alongside the Erebus in Melville Bay, and Sir John invited Captain Martin to dine with him, which the latter declined doing, as the wind was fair to go south; Sir John, while conversing with Captain Martin told him that he had five years provisions, which he could make last seven, and his people were busily engaged in salting down birds, of which they had several casks full already, and twelve men were out

shooting more. To see such determination and foresight
at that early period is really wonderful, and must give us
the greatest hopes.

I asked Captain Martin why he had not mentioned
this before ? He said that he did not at first think it of
any importance, and that when Lady Franklin was at
Peterhead about two years ago, he did not like to intrude
upon her Ladyship (not having the honour of knowing
her) during her short stay. He is a man of the strictest
integrity, whose word I can depend upon. He has an
independent fortune, which he got by fishing.

Your most obedient servant,

WILLIAM PENNY.

The remarkable statement of Captain Martin is
corroborated in a very striking manner by Mrs.
Blenky, who, in the following letter, addressed to
the " Morning Herald," gives an interesting extract
from the last communication she received from her
husband, a man of great experience, the ice-master
of the Terror, then in Baffin's Bay.

TO THE EDITOR OF THE " MORNING HERALD."

SIR,—Knowing the interest which is now felt in
the question of Sir John Franklin's long absence, I venture to offer you for publication in the " Morning

Herald," an extract from the last letter I received from my husband, who is ice-master on board the Terror, which will shew that they looked forward to the possibility of being detained much longer than had been generally supposed.

I may state that my husband was previously out with Sir John Ross in the Victory, when they were so many years missing. The letter was written on board the Terror at Disco Island, and is dated July 12th, 1845. He says:—" The season is a very open one, much such an one as when we came out with Captain Ross. We are all in good health and spirits, one and all appearing to be of the same determination, that is to persevere in making a passage to the North-west. Should we not be at home in the fall of 1848, or early in the spring of 1849, you may anticipate that we have made the passage, or likely to do so ; and if so, it may be from five to six years—it might be into the seventh—ere we return ; and should it be so, do not allow any person to dishearten you on the length of our absence, but look forward with hope that Providence will at length of time restore us safely to you."

I am, &c.,

ESTHER BLENKY.

21, *Hope-street, Liverpool, Feb.* 6, 1852.

I fear all this will be very heavy reading to some into whose hands this little book may probably fall. I have some hopes, however, that the reader who has had the patience to wade through these details will accompany us, perhaps not the less readily, through our Arctic journey, if he has been brought to share the conviction which animated my own mind in undertaking that division of the search which it is the object of the following pages to record—a conviction not in the least impaired by what I have seen and heard in the course of the last eighteen months, and which is simply this : that Franklin and his devoted companions have only not been heard of up to this time, because they have penetrated far beyond the reach of any means of relief, hitherto supplied to them. The field of search presented by the immense area of the Polar basin, compared with what has actually been accomplished in the way of examining it, is so vast, that any conclusion which would deprecate as hopeless all further inquiry into the fate of our missing countrymen, (resting upon the merely negative evidence of the absence of any trace or intelligence of them up to this time), is in my humble opinion, both premature and inconsiderate in the highest degree.

Not to digress, however, into a subject which would lead me much beyond the limits of an introductory chapter, it remains only to add (having traced the positive intelligence from the Expedition thus far, and shewn with what feelings they all appear to have been animated on entering upon their work) that the Erebus and Terror were seen once more, and for the last time, on the 26th July, 1845, by Captain Dannett of the whaler Prince of Wales. The ships were at that time in lat. 74° 48′ N., and long. 66° 13′ W. moored to an iceberg, and awaiting an opening in the middle ice to enable them to cross over to Lancaster Sound.

How, from that time to this, long weary years of conflicting anxiety and hope have elapsed without any tidings of them;—how the fair trust and confidence which followed their departure from England, became gradually darkened by a feeling of anxiety and uncertainty for their fate;—how vessel after vessel was despatched, in the vain effort (hitherto at least in vain) of affording them relief;—how un-

certainty gradually gave place to absurd and lying
tales, such as idle men and a somewhat too cre-
dulous public alone know how to propagate and to
receive :—all these things we know, and I need not
therefore occupy the reader's time in telling them.
Suffice it to say that in the fall of the year 1850, the
first ray of intelligence reached us of the movements
of the lost ones ; which, feeble as it was, and little of
positive information as it conveyed, was sufficient to
stir the heart of all England, shewing that her fears
had been premature, and setting at rest the then
prevailing opinion that the ships had foundered in
Baffin's Bay, 'ere they had even gained the entrance
of Lancaster Sound.

The Prince Albert, a little vessel fitted out by the
untiring devotion of Lady Franklin, assisted by the
liberality of a few private friends and public-spirited
philanthropists, had, after a remarkable voyage to the
Arctic seas, in the year 1850, brought back information of the discovery of traces of the missing Expedition at the entrance of Wellington Channel, which
left no doubt of their having passed the winter of
1845-6 in that neighbourhood. Without a moment's

hesitation, or count of the sacrifice of her already over-taxed means, Lady Franklin resolved to re-equip the Prince Albert for a second search; and from a number of volunteers for this noble service, I had the honour and privilege of being selected to command the Expedition, having the previous year made an offer of my services while residing in Canada.

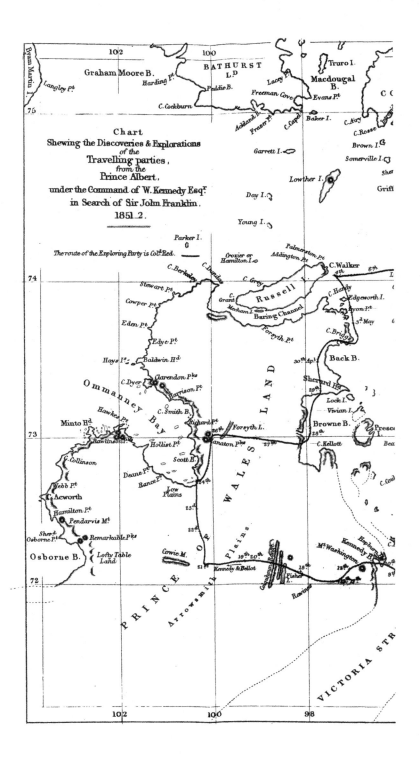

Chart
Shewing the Discoveries & Explorations
of the
Travelling parties,
from the
Prince Albert,
under the Command of W. Kennedy Esqr.
in Search of Sir John Franklin.
1851_2.

The route of the Exploring Party is Cold Red.

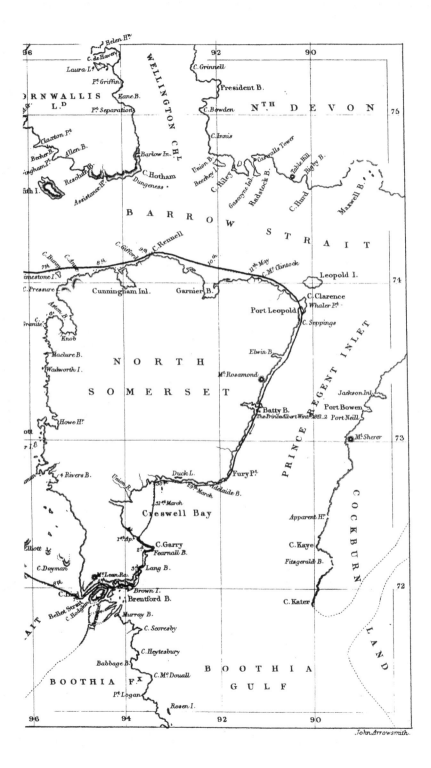

CHAPTER I.

FROM ABERDEEN TO CAPE FAREWELL.

"THE PRINCE ALBERT" FITTING OUT AT ABERDEEN
FOR HER SECOND VOYAGE TO THE POLAR SEAS—
STRENGTHENING FOR THE ICE — DESCRIPTION OF
THE CREW, AND STATEMENT OF THEIR AGES AND
PAY—LIEUT. BELLOT OF THE FRENCH NAVY AP-
POINTED SECOND IN COMMAND—ORGAN PRESENTED
BY H. R. H. PRINCE ALBERT—LEAVE ABERDEEN—
ARRIVAL AT THE ORKNEYS—CARRIER PIGEONS—
DEPARTURE FOR THE ARCTIC SEAS—OUR INSTRUC-
TIONS—SIGHT CAPE FAREWELL.

IT was a beautiful morning, on the 5th of May,
1851, when, after a smart run in the Royal Adelaide
from London, I found myself in the snug little
harbour of Aberdeen, pacing the deck of a small fairy-
looking craft, which might have been taken for a
yacht, or pleasure boat, intended for a summer cruize
along the picturesque shores of Scotland, but for
some unusual and queer-looking preparations which
were going on, on board of her. First, there was a

mysterious metamorphosis taking place in the upper
region of the main-mast, the effect of which, when
completed, was to convert a handsome symmetrical
little ketch, or schooner, into a rather awkward
top-heavy-looking Tom Thumb of a brig, of some
ninety tons burden. Along the sides, from the keel
to about two feet above the water line, there was
a doubling of American elm planking, two and a
half inches thick. The bows and stern post were
sheathed with wrought iron of about a quarter of an
inch in thickness, with a broad strip of thick sheet
iron along the water line as far aft as the foremast.
Her hold was a perfect labyrinth of cross-beams, one
set running across the vessel at distances of about ten
feet apart, midway between the kelson and the beams,
and another crossing these at right angles, and firmly
secured to the bottom and deck. The forepart of
the vessel had in addition what whalers call " poin-
ters," that is, a scantling, six inches square, running
from the kelson to midway up to the beams around
the larboard and port curves of the bow. It was
in fact the Prince Albert, fitting out for her proposed renewed search for Sir John Franklin, by way

of Prince Regent's Inlet—an important part of the
field of search for the missing Arctic Expedition,
which neither the squadron under Captain Austin's
orders, nor Captain Penny's expedition, at that time
engaged in the service, were able to provide for; and
which it was not to be expected that the American
Expedition, generously fitted out by Mr. Grinnell,
would undertake to perform.

While our sailing master Mr. John Leask (a veteran whaling captain, who had the previous winter filled
the post of ice-master in the North Star,) is engaged
in superintending these operations, let us introduce
you to our little ship's company. First, we have
from Aberdeen four stalwart fellows, who had sailed
with Captain Forsyth in the Albert's last voyage—
Henry Anderson, first mate; Robert Grate, boatswain; James Glennie, cook; and Alexander Matheson, able seaman. Next come three Shetlanders—
John Smith, who had also made the voyage, and
came with the highest recommendation for his
steady and faithful conduct, in consequence of which
he has now been appointed clerk in charge; his
brother, Gideon; and William Adamson, who had

accompanied Dr. Rae in his first journey to Repulse Bay. Richard Webb, a smart dashing fellow from London, who had accompanied Sir John Richardson in his boat journey through North America, goes out with us as engineer, in the event of our being able to make any use of the steam-launch, left by Sir James Ross at Port Leopold. Our carpenter is Kenneth Sutherland, six feet high, a *green hand*, in every sense of the term, who if not like Falstaff, a wit himself, is certainly like him destined throughout the voyage to be a cause of wit in others, but withal an honest, steady and industrious man. Four other veteran and hardy seamen, viz. Andrew Irvine, Magnus McCurrus, Andrew Linklater, and William Millar, afterwards to be shipped at Stromness in the Orkneys, will complete our complement of twelve excellent and experienced working hands.

Our muster-roll of officers is rather a large one. Mr. John Hepburn, a name familiar to Arctic voyagers, as the faithful attendant and sharer in the perils and privations of Sir John Franklin's first adventurous, and in some respects tragic journey

through North America, goes out in his old age, as
the best tribute he can render, of his affection for
his ancient commander; Mr. Robert Cowie, a member of a family I had long known and esteemed, has
kindly offered his services as Medical Officer to the
Expedition.* Together with those already mentioned,

* The following is a complete list of the crew, with their rank,
wages, and pay per month.

WM. KENNEDY, Commander.   J. BELLOT, second in command.

NAMES.	RANK.	AGE.	Wages per Month.			Wages per Annum.		
			£.	s.	d.	£.	s.	d.
John Leask . . .	Master . . .	56	12	0	0	144	0	0
John Hepburn . .	Supercargo .	62	10	0	0	120	0	0
Robt. Cowie . . .	Medical . .	27	4	3	4	50	0	0
John Smith . . .	Clerk in charge	30	5	0	0	60	0	0
Henry Anderson .	Chief Mate .	29	6	0	0	72	0	0
Kenneth Sutherland	Carpenter . .	28	5	0	0	60	0	0
Robert Grate . . .	Boatswain .	33	5	0	0	60	0	0
Richard Webb . .	Steward . .	28	6	0	0	72	0	0
James Glennie . .	Cook . . .	50	5	0	0	60	0	0
Alex. Matheson . .	Seaman . .	30	4	0	0	48	0	0
Wm. Adamson . .	,, . .	39	3	10	0	42	0	0
Gideon Smith . .	Blacksmith .	28	3	6	8	40	0	0
Andrew Irvine . .	Seaman : .	46	3	15	0	45	0	0
Andrew Linklater .	,, . .	47	3	15	0	45	0	0
Wm. Millar . . .	,, . .	33	3	0	0	36	0	0
Magnus McCurrus .	,, . .	45	3	0	0	36	0	0
			Per Annum, £			990	0	0

Besides the above wages the crew received, as gratuities, all the
clothing supplied them from the ship, and extra comforts, making
their entire remuneration considerably higher.

Mons. Bellot and myself, we have thus a total complement of eighteen in all.   Mons. Bellot is a young French naval officer distinguished in his own service, who has joined us as second in command, under circumstances so honourable to himself and to the gallant nation to which he belongs, that I make no apology for inserting here, with his permission, the generous offer of his services to Lady Franklin, which led to the securing of his invaluable co-operation in our little Expedition.

M. BELLOT TO MR. KENNEDY.

Rochefort sur Mer,
18th March, 1851.

Sir, —I am informed that you are about to command the Prince Albert. Since the inquiries about his (Sir John Franklin's) fate were begun, I always felt the greatest regret not to be in Europe to partake of the labours undergone by so many brave men that went in quest of the illustrious Lord Franklin. His Lordship's glory and success have made him a citizen of the world, and it is but justice that all seamen should take the most lively interest in his fate.

I would be peculiarly proud, Sir, to have your consent

to serving under your orders in such an honourable expedition. I have been now some years in the French service, and if zeal and devotedness may be relied upon, I can afford them to the greatest satisfaction of my wishes.

It would not be, for the first time, sharing fatigues and hard circumstances with English sailors, as I assisted to an action against the natives of Madagascar in 1848, in company of H. M. Frigate Conway; I was wounded there at the same time as Lieut. Kennedy, and wish he were a relative of yours. I wrote to our Navy Secretary for a leave of absence, and to Lady Franklin, but would not do so before warning you of it. I hope, Sir, there may be no objection to my being employed under your orders, and beg of you to give communication of my letter to Lady Franklin.

Please believe me, Sir,

Your most humble servant,

(Signed) J. BELLOT,

Lieut. French Navy, Knight of the Legion of Honour.

To this letter, after communicating with Lady Franklin and receiving her sanction, I made the following answer : her Ladyship having herself replied to the letter she had received from M. Bellot.

D

London, 1st of May, 1852.

DEAR SIR,

Your letter of the 18th March, conveying the generous offer of your services to Lady Franklin, to assist in the search for her gallant husband, unfortunately did not reach me here (owing to its being detained a considerable time at Aberdeen), until all the arrangements for the fitting out of the Prince Albert, and the appointing of her officers and men, had been completed.

I should inform you that the present expedition, like that of last year, is a private one, fitted out partly by subscription, but chiefly on the strength of the remaining resources of Lady Franklin herself.

Our little vessel measures only 90 tons, and her complement of officers and men, numbers only eighteen. If, however, after being made aware of these facts, you are still not entirely discouraged, and would like to witness our preparations, and to confer with me on the subject, you had better come over to England with the least possible delay. By inquiring at the Admiralty here for Mr. Barrow on your arrival, you would be instructed as to where to direct your steps.

In the enclosed document, which has been prepared and circulated by Lady Franklin's friends, with the view of promoting subscriptions in aid of her funds, you will find every information as to the means and objects of our contemplated undertaking.

I have much pleasure in forwarding you the accompanying number of the Morning Herald, one of the most respectable of our daily Journals, from which you will find that your gallant and generous offer has been duly recognized by the public sentiment of this country. As to myself I can only say with respect to it, that I look upon it as one of those noble deeds by which men alike distinguish themselves as individuals, and adorn the age in which they live, and that in having enlisted you, a member of the Legion of Honor, your nation have indeed chosen *un vrai Chevalier.*

I have the honor to be, &c.

WM. KENNEDY.

Lieut. J. Bellot.

P.S.—The vessel will sail from Aberdeen on the 15th of May.

To turn from this *coup d'œil* of our little company (a most satisfactory one at the time to myself, whatever it may be to the reader); let us return once more to the ship, and the state of her equipment for the arduous voyage on which she was about to enter.

The " Prince Albert," originally destined, I believe,
for the fruit trade, to and from the Azores, had
been purchased by Lady Franklin from Messrs.
White and Co. of Cowes, and sent to Aberdeen to
undergo additional strengthening and the alteration
of her rig under the hands of Mr. Duthie, the ship-
builder, for an Arctic voyage. Two splendid boats,
the one a gutta-percha boat, presented by the
Messrs. Searle of Lambeth, and the other a beautiful mahogany one, given by Messrs. White, were
attached to her from the previous voyage, besides
a Halkett's Mackintosh boat and a smaller kind
of boat called a dingey, sledges and kites. I had
long been of opinion that the search for Sir John
Franklin must ultimately resolve itself into a grand
series of boat and land journeys, and with this
view, after taking on board a supply of raw material,
for mocassins, snow-shoes, dog-sledges, &c. to be
worked up in the course of the voyage, I caused a
" kayack" to be constructed of tin, in imitation of
the native Esquimaux canoe ; intending, in the event
of our progress in the ship, or our own boats, being
arrested by any unforeseen circumstances, to adopt

the native method of travelling, with which, from many years residence among the Esquimaux of Labrador, I was perfectly familiar. By the liberality of the Admiralty, we were supplied with a ton and a half of excellent pemmican, which proved invaluable in the extensive winter journeys we were afterwards called upon to undertake. No expense was spared in furnishing us with everything else considered necessary for the particular service we were to be engaged upon. Provisions, in full quantity, and in the providing of which no expense had been spared, were placed on board, amply sufficient for two years. The means of communicating with our good friends in England were not overlooked among our other preparations for the voyage. A relay of couriers, fit for the service of an Emperor, and warranted free from the annual " Christmas-box" imposition of their confreres of St. Martin's le Grand, were secured for the special department of the Post-office of the Prince Albert, in the shape of six carrier pigeons supplied to us by the liberality of Mr. Hodgson of Kennington, with one who had precedence of the rest, coming to us with the style and title of " Lady

Ross," from Miss Dunlop of Annan Hill of Ayrshire. Lastly, our little vessel was honoured by the gift of an organ from His Royal Highness Prince Albert, of which the value, great as it was to us on our long and dreary voyage, was enhanced by the gracious terms in which the favour was conveyed.

Having completed our preparations by the 22nd May, the Prince Albert left Aberdeen harbour at six o'clock P.M. with the Union jack flying at the peak, and the French flag at the fore, in honour of our gallant comrade Bellot, and at four A.M. on the 25th she came safely to anchor off Stromness, after carrying away the jib-boom on the same morning, off Duncansby Head during a squall. Lady Franklin, Miss Sophia Cracroft, and myself had in the meantime gone round by the steamer by way of Kirkwall, where, as well as at Stromness, we left behind us many pleasing recollections of the genuine and unaffected kindness and hospitality everywhere shewn by these warm-hearted islanders.

By the 3rd of June we were once more ready for sea. And now came the usual hurry and bustle of departure. Last letters were written—last visits paid, and Jack's last farewells to Robina and Maggie, fairly got over, when the order was given for all hands on board. There, in our little cabin with her estimable neice, sat the truly feminine yet heroic spirit who presided over our gallant little enterprise, one whose name—if her husband's is already associated with the highest honours of geographical discovery—will not be the less so hereafter in the hearts of Englishmen, with honours of another kind—the most noble, devoted, and unwearied efforts to rescue or solve the fate of our missing countrymen.

One by one each of our little party was introduced, and cheered by her words of wise and affectionate counsels. If ever three English cheers were given with the heart's best feelings of a British sailor, they were given, when stepping over the vessel's side, our noble patroness waved us her last adieu and God's blessing on our voyage.

*   *   *   *   *   *
*   *   *   *   *   *

And now for the North-west, we exclaimed, as at two P.M. on the 3rd June, with flags flying, and a lovely garland woven by the fair hands of the ladies of

Stromness and of Wolverhampton, to hang to our shrouds, we hoisted anchor to the *refrain* of the time-worn seaman's ditty of the " Girls we left behind us," and proceeded to sea by Hoy Sound. About four P.M., while off Hoy Head, we were somewhat astonished to find one of our pigeons sitting quietly in the rigging. During the hurry of our departure, it had escaped unperceived, and it had now by a remarkable exercise of instinct followed us to sea and rejoined its companions. Two bottles, containing papers addressed to Mr. Wylie, our agent at Stromness, giving notice of its recovery were immediately thrown overboard. One of them, we have since learned, was picked up four days after at Rapness, Westray, one of the northernmost of the Orkney Islands.

While the Prince Albert is proceeding rapidly forward with a succession of delightful weather towards Cape Farewell, let us take a cursory glance at our instructions. We knew nothing at this time, it must be remembered, of the movements of Captains Austin's and Penny's squadrons, nor of the discoveries in Wellington Channel, and the lands to the South and West of Cape Walker. The locality allotted for our search included Prince Regent's Inlet, and the passages connecting it with the Western Sea, S.W. of Cape Walker, to which latter quarter Sir John Franklin, as will have been seen by his instructions, was required in the first instance to proceed.

This search was assumed to be necessary on the following grounds.

1. The probability of Sir John Franklin having abandoned his vessels to the south-west of Cape Walker.

2. The fact that, when Franklin sailed, he believed that an open passage was to be found from the westward into the south part of Regent's Inlet, according to the chart supplied to him from the Admiralty, and which does not exhibit the discoveries of Rae, made subsequently to that period.

3. Sir John Franklin would, it was thought, be more likely to take this course, through the country known to possess the resources of animal life, with the wreck of the Victory in Felix Harbour for fuel, and the stores at Fury Beach, farther north in view,

than to fall back upon an utterly barren region of the north coast of America.

4. He would be more likely to expect succour to be sent to him by way of Lancaster Sound, and Barrow's Straits, into which Regent's Inlet opens, than in any other direction.

How the discoveries of Captain Penny in Wellington Channel had rendered it almost certain that Franklin had selected that route, in preference to any other; and how far the explorations of Captains Ommanney and Osborn had anticipated us to some extent, even in our own field of search, I know *now*, but would have given my right hand to have know *then*. " *L'homme propose, et Dieu dispose.*"

Lady Franklin's anxiety for the search of Wellington Channel was well known, and indeed it was not until she felt this object to be secured by the instructions to Captain Austin and Captain Penny that she directed her little vessel to this auxiliary search, which in the entire uncertainty which then existed, appeared of great importance, and on former occasions had entered into the Admiralty instructions, though never acted upon.

In the mean time we are rapidly approaching the coast of Greenland. Sunday, the 24th June, at four P.M., the land of Cape Farewell, bearing east, and distant about forty miles, was distinctly seen, and the first stage of our outward journey was over, after having had scarcely a day of what could be called bad weather, and with no other misadventure than a thorough good shaking in one or two rough squalls in the North Atlantic.

CHAPTER II.

THE coast of Greenland has little in its appearance
to interest an ordinary observer. A gaunt, sterile,
iron-bound shore, meets the eye in every direction,
relieved only by huge masses of sheer perpendicular

cliff rising sternly into the sky, often more than a
thousand feet high.   Here and there the gloomy,
cavernous portal of some deep fiord, running many
miles into the land, sends forth, ever and anon, its
monstrous spawn of ice-bergs surging lazily through
the dark green waters.   Rarely—very rarely—the
eye rests delightedly upon some sunny spot of ver-
dure, all the more lovely for the surrounding desolation, where some wandering Vikingr of old—the hero
of some forgotten Saga—might have set up his rest,
on his journey to the sunny Vinland.*   But bleak-
ness, barrenness, and famine, this is the general
aspect, and anything but an inviting-looking foretaste
it was of what we were to expect in those regions of
"thick-ribbed ice," of which we were as yet but
entering upon the threshold.   *N'importe.*   "A stout
heart," as they say in Scotland, "always to a steep
brae."

*   *   *   *   *   *

Cape Farewell is already some hundred miles
behind, and we are rapidly picking up those quaint

---

* The old Icelandic name of America—the discovery of which, by
the Northmen of Greenland, long prior to the time of Columbus, is
now no longer a question admitting of dispute.

old names, " Cape Desolation," (which, as the gallant
Fitzjames remarked as he passed it, sounds polar
enough), " Cape Comfort," " Sanderson his Hope,"
—the suggestive and touching memorials of the
struggling and patient heroism of our early Arctic
Navigators.

> " And now there came both mist and snow,
> And it grew wond'rous cold,
> And ice, mast high, came floating by
> As green as emerald.
> Through drifts the snowy cliffs
> Did send a dismal sheen ;
> Nor shapes of men or beasts we ken,
> The ice was all between.
> With sloping masts and dripping prow,
> As who pursued with yell and blow,
> Still treads the shadow of his foe,
> And forward bends his head.
> The ship drove past—loud roared the blast,
> And *northward* aye we fled."

On Tuesday the 8th July, we were three-fourths
of the way up Baffin's Bay, and nearly opposite
the little Danish colony of Upernavik.

We had this morning been visited by Captains
Patterson and Walker, of the whaling ships " Pacific"
of Aberdeen, and " Jane" of Bo'ness, who breakfasted

with us, and brought with them a document which set our little society in a ferment. It was headed, "Memorandum of traces of Sir John Franklin's Expedition," and was to the following purport.

"1st. Three graves, neatly made, with wooden head-boards, bearing the names of,

"Wm. Braine, R.M. H.M.S. 'Erebus,' April 3, 1846, Æt. 32.

"John Hartnell, A.B., H.M.S. 'Erebus.' Æt. 25.

"John Torrington, Jan. 1st. H.M.S. 'Terror.' Æt. 20.

"2nd. An anvil stand with remnant of coals, &c. indications of the armourer's forge.

"3rd. A large mound, with marked evidence of the carpenter's saw, observatory, and perhaps a shore store house.

"4th. Scraps of clothing, canvas, cordage and papers, scattered over a large area, comprehended between Capes Riley and Spencer. Stacks of preserved meat cans were found.

"The graves and remnants of winter-quarters were grouped upon a sloping neck of land, to the N.E. of Beechey Island. The indentation between Cape

Riley and Beechey Island was the probable seat of
the missing Expedition's first winter harbour.

(Signed)   E. W. KANE, U.S.N.

" *Baffin's Bay, off Upernavik,*
July 7th, 1851."

This paper was given to Captain Walker by Dr.
Kane of the Advance, who informed him that these
" traces " had been found by Captain Penny, of the
" Lady Franklin," in September last.

About eleven A.M. our visitors returned to their
ships, taking with them despatches for England,
enclosing a copy of the above information.   They
stated to us that the American discovery vessels,
" Advance" and " Rescue," had wintered in the
pack, and were, probably, at this time not far off, as
indeed was evident from the dating of the memorandum.   We lost no time, therefore, on receipt of this
deeply-interesting intelligence, in bearing up for
Upernavik, with the view partly of taking in some
supplies for the use of our winter travelling parties;
but mainly in the hope of finding farther information there from the Americans, in which latter expectation, however, we were doomed to be disappointed.

Upernavik, which we reached on the morning of
the 10th, is, as every one knows, one of that interesting group of little colonies with which the enterprise
of the Danes has dotted the west coast of Greenland.
It was, perhaps, natural in one who had recently
come from a British possession, in some respects
analogous, although infinitely superior in produc-
tiveness and capability of improvement—I mean the
territories around Hudson's Bay—to take some interest in these remarkable and unique examples of
colonizing 'under difficulties.' My first impression
was certainly one of gratified surprise that here,
considerably within the Arctic Circle, (within a degree
or two in fact of the entrance of Wellington Channel,
where Franklin had he remained, must, according to
some lugubrious authorities, have long ago perished
of starvation,) there was a Christian community, not
only living but after a fashion, thriving.   We were
informed by the Governor that there was even at this
early period of the season, one thousand Danish tuns
of oil and blubber stored, from the produce of the
summer fishery.   There was likewise visible evidence
in every direction of an abundance of venison, water-

E

fowl and eggs, as well as seals. The houses were built of wood, very small, and had a singularly amphibious look about them, from being covered with tar from top to bottom, looking for all the world like so many upturned herring-boats, ready on any emergency to take to the water.

A party of the Esquimaux, attached to the settlement, had come in with the produce of some hunting excursion in which they had been engaged, and I was much struck with their intelligence, and their well-clad comfortable and healthy appearance. This I learned was in a great measure due to the benevolent interest of the Danish Government in their behalf. There is not a station, I was given to understand, along the whole coast of Greenland which has not its missionary and its schoolmaster for the instruction of the natives ; and judging from what we saw and learned at Upernavik, the Danish exchequer is not without material and substantial proofs of the gratitude of the poor " *Innuit*." Thus instructed, cared for, and their energies disciplined and directed, the Esquimaux of Greenland give employment, as I am informed, to six ships annually,

in carrying the produce of their hunts and fisheries
to Denmark.

We took on board at Upernavik six powerful
Esquimaux dogs, and a few pairs of sealskin boots,
shoes, and trousers for the use of our travelling
parties, and, bidding adieu to our hospitable friends,
resumed our course northward.

On the 13th, as we had expected, we fell in with
the American squadron, at that time all well and in
high spirits, after their extraordinary and unparalleled
drift of eight months in the heart of the pack, through
Lancaster Sound and Baffin's Bay. We kept together
till the 4th of August, making a few miles northing
generally every day by incessantly watching every
opening in the close packed ice, but on arriving off
the "Devil's Thumb," a name more quaint than all
preceding names, where Melville Bay commences,
we found it completely blocked up. Farther progress in this direction being judged impracticable,
we determined to attempt a passage farther south.
Leaving the Americans in about lat. 74° 30' we
accordingly proceeded southward, and struck the
middle ice in lat. 72° N. and after four days of most

difficult and perilous navigation succeeded in effecting a passage through one hundred and twenty miles of densely packed ice, reaching the " west water " on the 21st August. We judged this a proper opportunity for testing the powers of our carrier-pigeons; but after letting them all off in succession we found that no coaxing could induce them to leave the ship. Some would alight in the rigging, others would fly a few hundred yards and settle on the ice; but they invariably found their way back to the vessel. " Lady Ross," the bird which is said on a former occasion to have been dispatched from Lancaster Sound and to have arrived safe at its former home in Scotland, though without credentials of its identity or its mission, was reserved for a special emergency, namely, to announce the discovery of Sir John Franklin, should that happy fortune befal us. I must, therefore, in common chivalry, except her from this account, which must be considered as leaving *her* fair fame untarnished to the last. According to the usual practice we had secured a considerable portion of our provisions on deck on reaching Melville Bay, in case of shipwreck. These were now stowed away once more into the hold, the most dangerous part of the navigation being now considered as fairly past. Our passage on the whole was a most fortunate one. The much and justly dreaded middle-ice, which has been the grave of many a goodly craft, had been passed without a single accident—not even one of those romantic " *nips* " which figure so dramatically in the narratives of our predecessors. In this respect, the very Lilliputian dimensions of the Prince Albert, upon which some croakers in England had founded their predictions of our going to the bottom, were, I cannot help thinking, under Providence, our greatest security.

Tuesday, August 26th.—Found ourselves, after a fine run through comparatively open water, off Pond's Bay. We were here for the first and last time during our voyage visited by a small party of four Esquimaux, who reported, having seen some ' moons' previously two ships proceeding southward, which I have reason to believe could have been no other than the American Squadron, while drifting down Lancaster Sound in the pack. Our Chancellor of the Exchequer, Mr. John Smith, having some acquaintance with the Esquimaux language, contrived to extract some useful information from our visitors, who were, to do them justice, disposed to be friendly and communicative to the utmost of their power. One of them, who seemed to have a turn for hydrography, or at any rate had used his eyes to some purpose during his travels, drew with a piece of chalk on the deck, a very correct delineation of the Inlet, leading out of Pond's Bay as far as Navy Board Inlet, and again of Admiralty Inlet for a considerable distance inland.

Having extracted what we could from them in the shape of news, the idea struck some metaphysical mind of our party to try the effect of "music on the savage breast." Accordingly the organ was brought on deck and set going, and its effect, whatever it may be in poetry, was anything but "soothing" upon our visitors. From the first, it was evidently regarded as possessed of some mysterious powers of life and volition, which they acknowledged by dancing and singing around it in the most uproarious manner. One poor fellow was particularly distinguished by the oddity and extravagance of his behaviour. At the first note he was observed to

" grin horribly a ghastly smile,"—this was followed
by a whoop, and a yell, and a leap in the air; as if he
were possessed by a legion of demons; and so he
went on leaping, and howling, and using all the
frantic gesticulations of a madman, till in mercy to
the poor creature's wits, we were forced to stop the
organ and his extacies together.

A singular atmospheric phenomenon may be
mentioned "en passant," in connection with this
visit of the Esquimaux, proving the highly conduc-
tive properties of the atmosphere in these latitudes
under certain conditions. Long before they reached
the vessel, their voices, and even their well known
salutation " CHIMO," could be plainly distinguished,
although at a distance which we estimated could not
have been under six or eight miles.

From Pond's Bay, we had upon the whole a
favourable passage through Lancaster Sound, in spite
of some strong easterly gales, which raised a very
heavy and dangerous swell among the loose ice, to
avoid which it was necessary to keep the vessel
continually dodging and tacking, off and on, across
the Sound. It was the 3rd of September before we

were sufficiently advanced through Barrow's Straits, to attempt putting our long cherished resolution of visiting Cape Riley in search of the traces of Sir John Franklin, already described, into execution; but.after repeatedly bearing up for the North Land, through heavy fogs, alternating with showers of rain and snow, with continued heavy gales from the East and North-east, we found that the dense accumula. tion of ice, rendered farther progress in this direction altogether hopeless. It was part of our instructions to touch if possible at Griffiths Island, where information of the movements of the searching squadron under Captain Austin and Captain Penny, had been directed to be deposited, but the long continuance of easterly gales had driven all the loose ice up the Sound, and on arriving off Port Leopold we found Barrow's Straits, barred from side to side.

Thursday, Sept. 4th.—Leopold Island, about ten miles to the north of Leopold Harbour, which will be familiar to Arctic readers, as the winter-quarters of Sir James Ross's Expedition in 1848-49, lay close on our weather bow. An unbroken barrier of ice, similar to that observed in Barrow's Straits, could

be distinctly traced, extending as far as the eye
could reach down the west side of Prince Regent's
Inlet, piled up in a dense mass on the shore, while
the east side and middle of the Inlet were comparatively open.

This will be readily understood as the effect of the
long continuance of easterly winds, and we were still
in hopes, that the mischief thus done, a change of
wind to an opposite direction might as readily undo.
With the view of watching the desired change in a
situation where advantage could be instantly taken of
a favourable movement of the ice, we resolved to run
into Leopold Harbour. To our great disappointment
we found the entrance completely blocked up. An
attempt was made by Mr. Bellot, four men and
myself to effect a landing in the gutta-percha boat,
but without success. The ice was found in a state
of terrific agitation, threatening certain destruction
to either boat or ship which should attempt a passage
through it. We then ran down to Elwin Bay, but
found it closed; next to Batty Bay, and found it
the same; then to Fury Beach, when, perceiving
ourselves in the same situation which led to the

wreck of the Fury, namely, in a narrow lane between an extensive field of moving ice and the shore, we judged it prudent to beat a retreat without loss of time. The entire west shore being thus closed against us, no alternative remained but to run for the opposite side of the Inlet, which being sheltered from this pestilent east gale, was free from ice altogether. Accordingly after a circuit of some forty hours, along a dead wall of ice, we brought up in Port Bowen, in the evening of the 5th. We remained here two days. Mr. Bellot and myself landed on the island at the entrance of the harbour and afterwards on the mainland, and found the following traces of the party who wintered with Sir E. Parry in the locality; viz. *on the island,* a cairn built on the highest point—a large kiln-like fire-place on the N.E. side, where, apparently, lime had been burned, a small strip of canvas in good preservation, some nails and pieces of broken pipes; on *the mainland,* two cairns and a grave, with a small hut-like house, solid in every part, built on the top of it, with the following inscription cut on a stone forming part of the west gable : —

" The body of John Cottrell, seaman of H.M.S. Fury, is hereunder deposited, who was unfortunately drowned on the 6th of July, 1825, in the 39th year of his age."

Mr. Bellot, with a boat's crew, visited Port Neill, but found no traces of any kind beyond an old Esquimaux encampment. It would clearly never do to winter in Port Bowen, while all our work lay upon the other side of the Inlet. It was resolved, therefore, at all hazards, to make another attempt to reach Port Leopold, where it was desirable, at any rate, to effect a landing, in order to ascertain whether any intelligence had been left there by Captain Austin or Captain Penny. Accordingly, on the evening of the 9th, having re-crossed the inlet, and succeeded in bringing the ship to within a couple of miles of Cape Seppings (the south point of Port Leopold), I determined once more to make the experiment of landing with the boat, the entrance to the harbour being still deemed impracticable for the ship. Taking four of the crew, Alexander Matheson, Gideon Smith, Andrew Irvine, and Kenneth Sutherland, in the gutta-percha boat, I left the ship about seven

P.M., and was fortunate enough to find a narrow lane of water which brought us, without any difficulty, to the shore. On ascending the high cliff of Cape Seppings, I had the satisfaction of seeing the harbour quite free from ice, and if the ship could retain her position for a few hours longer, I had every reason to believe that a passage might be safely effected, by taking advantage of the movements of the ice, through the slight barrier which still blocked up the entrance. After an hour's reconnoitring we prepared to rejoin the vessel; but found our return cut off by the ice, which had, in the meantime, as I afterwards learned, embayed the Prince Albert in a sort of pool, and here we were all drifting to the southward in a body down the Inlet. To add to our perplexity, night had come on. Nothing could be seen or heard around us but huge masses of ice, grinding, tossing, and rearing furiously on every side. To attempt to reach the ship under such circumstances was to ensure certain destruction to the boat and every body in it; and nothing was left, therefore, but to return to the shore, which we succeeded in reaching in safety, about two miles to the south

SEPARATION FROM THE SHIP AT CAPE SEPPINGS

COVENTRY LITH

of Cape Seppings. Drawing our boat up on the
beach, and turning her up as a shelter from the
night air, we prepared to pass the night under
her as we best could. The weather was bitterly
cold; our clothes were little else than a mass
of ice, and knowing, under such circumstances, the
danger of allowing the men to fall asleep, I permitted each of them to take an hour's *rest*, in turn,
under the boat, but no more; and kept them for the
remainder of the night in active exercise. With the
dawn of the following morning we scrambled to the
highest cliff of Cape Seppings, stiff, cold, and weary;
and the consternation of the poor men may be con-
ceived on discovering that every vestige of the Prince
Albert had disappeared during the night.

I was not without my own fears of the issue of
this adventure, more however as regarded the ship
than ourselves, as we could always fall back, in case
of emergency, upon the provisions deposited by Sir
James Ross at Whaler Point, on the other side of
the harbour. Thither we now directed our steps, and
fortunately found the depôt precisely in the condition
in which it had been left two years before, with the

exception of a cask of tallow which had been emptied by the bears and foxes, a case of chocolate partly destroyed, and a cask of biscuit much damaged. The house erected by Sir James Ross was still standing, but the covering much injured. A cylinder attached to the flagstaff contained a notice of the deposit of provisions, and of his future intentions.

The notices left by Mr. Saunders and by Commander Forsyth were also in the same cylinder, but these being printed in the Parliamentary Reports need not be transcribed.

It was evident from this that neither Sir John Franklin, nor any of the other Government vessels had touched here since it was last visited by the Prince Albert in the previous autumn.

It was now the 10th of September—winter was evidently fast setting in—and from the distance the ship had been carried during that disastrous night, (whether out to sea or down the Inlet we could not conjecture), there was no hope of our being able to rejoin her at least during the present season. There remained, therefore, no alternative but to make up our minds to pass the winter, if necessary, where we were.

I pass over the anguish of the reflection at such a termination to our enterprise, so full as we had been of hope and confidence, and determination to accomplish the duty that had been assigned to us. The reader will not fail to feel a little interest even in a feeling so deeply personal, but the humble companions of my misfortune occupied with the considerations of their own safety during the long and dreary winter that was before them, could hardly be expected to find room for other thoughts.

It was a relief, therefore, to my own sorrowful contemplations to begin to discuss with them with as much cheerfulness as I could command, our little plans for our future proceedings. The first object to be attended to, was the erecting of some sort of shelter against the daily increasing inclemency of the weather, and for this purpose the launch, left here by Sir James Ross, was selected. Her mainmast was laid on supports at the bow and stern, about nine feet in height, and by spreading two of her sails over this a very tolerable roof was obtained. A stove was set up in the body of the boat with the pipes running through the roof, and we were soon sitting by a comfortable fire, which after our long exposure to the wet and cold we stood very much in need of. There was a plentiful supply of blanket bags in the depôt, by the aid of which we were soon in possession of as warm and comfortable bedding as we could desire. Out of the same material we were able to supply ourselves with some excellent clothing, using, in the absence of ordinary needles and thread, sail needles and twine, which answered our purpose equally well. These and other preparations of a similar nature carried us through the first week of our dreary residence with a very tolerable approach to comfort and contentment.

The following extracts from the rough notes of my Journal at Whaler Point will perhaps convey a more accurate idea of the routine of our daily life for the rest of the period of our detention there, than any mere formal description.

Sunday, 21st Sept. —We were able to enjoy a day of rest, after a severe and laborious week of exertion. It was a pleasing sight, in the absence of the regular means for conducting the exercises appropriate to the day, to observe how the men were occupied in

recalling to mind some of the sacred melodies of
their native land, and the simple hymns, stored up
in their memories from childhood, as well as those
exquisite cullings from the word of truth, embodied
in the Shorter Catechism of the Church of Scotland.

Monday, 21st. — No appearance of the Prince
Albert, and our last lingering hopes, of her being
able to gain Leopold Harbour, once more before the
winter finally sets in — a hoping against hope to
which men in our situation are perhaps naturally
prone—are fast disappearing. Our own most press-
ing personal wants being now provided for, as far
as under our present circumstances this can be done,
we are more at liberty to discuss plans of operation
for the coming winter and spring. My present
intention is, as soon as the state of the ice will admit
of travelling parties being sent out, to institute a
strict search for the ship, in every direction in which
we can suppose her likely to have been carried, and in
the event of this being unsuccessful, to commence early
in the spring a journey to Cape Walker, with the view
of carrying into effect, as far as our limited means will
allow, the great object for which we have been sent

F

out, of discovering traces of Sir John Franklin. To attempt a long journey as I had once hoped, in the dead of winter, is utterly impossible from the wretched state of our equipment in regard to clothing. Our greatest deficiency is in the article of shoes, for which we have no other material than the old canvas housing of the building, erected here by Sir James Ross, which constant exposure to the weather has very much deteriorated. It will be the constant occupation of two men for some weeks to provide a stock of shoes of this material, (which we find wears out in a few days,) for the use of the travelling parties, before any very extended excursion can be undertaken.

Friday, Oct. 3rd. — Kenneth Sutherland, the carpenter, was set to-day to prepare some wood for snow-shoe frames and for a winter sleigh on the Esquimaux model. Being much annoyed by smoke every morning when our fires are lighted, in consequence of the small calibre of the stove-pipes (metal tube $2\frac{1}{2}$ inches in diameter), Gideon Smith was set to cut up a preserved potato case, which he has converted into wider pipes, which are found to be a great improvement on the old ones.

Saturday, 4th.—Our winter sleigh being completed was tried and found to answer pretty well. It is three feet four inches in length by eight inches wide. The runners which are five inches deep, are shod with frozen dough after the Equimaux fashion, then planed quite smooth and coated over by the hand with water, which immediately congeals into a smooth glassy surface which enables it to run over the snow with great ease.

Tuesday, 7th.—While the carpenter was employed in converting a refractory piece of sandstone into a grind-stone, two men and self proceeded to the shores of Barrow's Straits in order to examine the state of the ice in that direction. Found a signal post erected by a party from Sir James Ross. To the pole, which had been much gnawed by bears up to one-third of its height, was attached a cylinder, with a notice, intimating, for the information of Sir John Franklin, that a depot of provisions had been left at Whaler Point by the expedition under Sir James Ross, and his future course.

Tuesday, 14th. — A few hours after sun-rise, observed one of those remarkable solar phonomena,

F 2

seen only I believe in the Arctic regions. A magnificent luminous circle was observed round the sun, about 45 degrees in diameter, and intersected by two broad belts of resplendent light, at right angles to each other, broadest in the centre and tapering at both ends to a point. Altogether a truly magnificent spectacle.

Some bears and foxes are seen occasionally prowling about our residence, attracted probably by the odour of our *cuisine*. Instituted a general chase after a large bear, but was unsuccessful.

Thursday, 17th.—Towards evening, heard a shot in the direction of Cape Seppings, and on looking out found it to proceed from a party of seven men under Mr. Bellot, who had dragged the jolly boat of the Prince Albert all the way from Batty Bay. It was with emotions of inexpressible thankfulness and joy that we received the intelligence that the entire party were well, and that the Prince Albert was safely moored in a good position in Batty Bay.

I cannot refrain, from recording here, my warmest thanks to Mr. Bellot, not only for this, but two other attempts which he had made to communicate to us

the intelligence of the Prince Albert's position, and
to bring us a supply of clothing. He had set out
with two men to come by land to Port Leopold, the
third day after getting into Batty Bay, but after three
days' march, over the wild and rugged hills, wading
through deep snow, and walking against continual
drift, they were obliged to return to the ship after
much suffering from cold and wet. He next made a
gallant attempt alongshore by means of dogs and
sledges, but getting on weak ice, fell through, and had
again to return with the loss of a sledge and part of
its contents. The third (the present) attempt was
more successful. The little boat, as already stated,
had been dragged all the way, in the event of any
occasion arising for its use where the ice had not
formed. They found the ice, however, formed all
the way to this point, and in many places so rough,
that they had often to drag their boat over points of
land.

On this last occasion of his setting out from the
Prince Albert, M. Bellot addressed the following letter
to Lady Franklin, which, as indicative of the gallant

determination with which the journey was undertaken, I consider it but due to him to insert.

Prince Albert, Batty Bay,

12th of October, 1851.

MADAM,

Having failed in my first undertaking to rescue
our dear Mr. Kennedy and the absent party, I am to
start again to renew our attempt, accompanied by the
doctor and two hands. I am fully aware both of the
hazard of such a trip at this time of the year, and of its
consequences on the future prospect of the Expedition,
should we be destined not to return. Whatever it may
be, I hope I need not make any apology of my motives ;
for being convinced of what importance is Mr. Kennedy's presence in our next operations, and remembering
your strong recommendations to hazard every thing for
any man's life,* I think that in the present unforeseen
circumstances, it would be grossly mistaking your Ladyship's intentions, not to obey the advices of our duty as
ship-mates, and of humanity as fellow-men, even though
we should perhaps risk the success of the chief purpose

* Lady Franklin had recommended, never to risk any man's life,
even if it should be at the cost of the Prince Albert herself.

which we are sent out on ; were it God's blessed will not to make fruitful our endeavours. Being moved in all my determinations by the strongest wishes of not sparing any effort for your Ladyship's service, I beg you will consider me as your Ladyship's

Most respectful and devoted servant,

(Signed) J. BELLOT.

CHAPTER III.

IT can hardly be a matter of surprise that the re-
action in the state of our feelings, consequent upon
this unexpected meeting with our long-lost friends,
should have been striking and immediate, and in
direct proportion to our former solicitude and dejec-
tion.

It was but five weeks "by the chime" since our
disastrous separation from the Prince Albert; but
they were five *years* of dreary anxiety and despon-

dency, fast merging into something like despair. We had a jovial evening, let the reader be well assured, in our little launch that 17th of October, and a jovial house-warming, out of Her Majesty's stores at Port Leopold, enjoyed none the less from the absence of any grim vision of a long reckoning to discharge with "mine host" on the morrow. And we kept it up too, let me tell you, with long yarns of our adventures, and rough old sea songs; and in brimming cups of famous chocolate, "cheering but not inebriating," drank most loyally (at Her Majesty's expense) a happy meeting with H.M.S. Erebus and Terror, and their gallant crews.

It was some days after this before our preparations for returning to the ship were completed. At last, on Wednesday the 22nd, exactly six weeks after our first detention at Whaler Point, we set out; after depositing a paper in the cylinder, containing information of our proceedings up to this date, and placing all the loose stores in proper order and security for the use of any party that should come after us.

Our provisions and 'traps' of all kinds were stowed in the boat, and the whole secured on a strong sleigh.

A mast was then set, and a sail hoisted in the jolly boat, and away we went before a spanking fair wind over the smooth ice of Leopold harbour, at a rate which " all the king's horses " could hardly have been equal to. We had not gone half across the bay, however, before our sleigh, wholly unused to this style of locomotion, broke down, and it cost us the best part of the day, before we could repair our damages and start afresh.

In the endeavour to reach Mr. Bellot's encampment of the 16th, we continued on foot longer than we should have done, and the consequence was, that being overtaken by night before looking for camping ground, we found ourselves, before we were aware or had time to reflect on the predicament we had got into, groping about, in the darkness, and with a heavy shower of snow falling, for some bit of terra firma, (for we had been all day upon the ice), where we could pitch the tent. We stumbled at last, after making our shins more freely acquainted than was altogether agreeable with the sharp edges of the broken ice, into a fine square space of clear beach, between some heavy masses of stranded ice. Choosing

out the softest part of a shelving rock of limestone of
which the beach was composed, we pitched the tent,
spread the oil-cloth, and with some coals, which we
had brought with us from Whaler Point, boiled a
good kettle of tea for all hands.

All these preparations were, however, but introductory to another, which we found a most difficult
problem indeed—namely, to contrive how we were all
to pass the night in the single little tent we had
brought with us.   We all got in, certainly, and got
the kettle in the middle; but as for lying down to
sleep, it was utterly out of the question.   A London
omnibus, on a racing day after five o'clock, was the
only parallel I could think of to our attempt to stow
thirteen men, including our colossal carpenter, into
a tent intended for six.   At last, after some deliberation, it was arranged that we should sit down six in
a row, on each side, which would leave us about three
feet clear to stretch our legs.   Mr. Bellot, who
formed the thirteenth, being the most compact and
stowable of the party, agreed to squeeze in underneath them, stipulating only for a clear foot square
for his head alongside the tea-kettle.   Being unpro-

vided with a candlestick, even if there had been room
to place one anywhere, it was arranged that each of
us should hold the candle in his hand for a quarter
of an hour, and then pass it to his neighbour, and
thus by the aid of our flickering taper, through the
thick steam of the boiling kettle, we had just enough
light to prevent us putting our tea into our neighbour's mouth, instead of our own.

"Well, boys," suggests our ever jovial first mate,
Henry Anderson, "now we are fairly seated, I'm
thinking, as we can do nothing else, we had best
make a night of it again. What say you to a song,
Dick?" Whereupon, nothing loath, Mr. Richard
Webb strikes up, in the first style of forecastle execution, "Susannah, don't you cry for me," which is of
course received by the company with the utmost
enthusiasm. "Mr. Webb, your health and song,"
and general applause, and emptying of tea-cans,
which Mr. John Smith, pleading inability to sing,
undertakes to replenish for the night.

"Irvine, my lad, pass the candle, and give us the
'Tailor.'" Mr. Irvine, you must understand, gentle
reader, has distinguished himself by some extraordi-

nary performances on the blanket-bags, during our late detention at Whaler Point, in virtue of which he has been formally installed "Tailor to the Expedition."

"The Tailor" is accordingly given, *con amore*, and is a remarkable history of a knight of the thimble, who, burying his goose, like Prospero his books, "beyond the reach of plummet," becomes "a sailor bold," and in that capacity enslaves the heart of a lovely lady of incalculable wealth, who, &c. &c. — We all know the rest.

"Kenneth, you monster, take that clumsy foot of yours off my stomach, will you?" cries out poor Mr. Bellot, smothered beneath the weight of four-and-twenty legs, upon which the carpenter, in his eagerness to comply, probably drives his foot into Mr. Bellot's eye.

And so, passing the song and the joke around— Mr. Bellot, occasionally making a sudden desperate effort to get up, and settling down again in despair— with a long "blow" like a grampus—we make what Anderson calls "a night of it." No management, however, can make our solitary candle last out beyond twelve o'clock, or thereabout. Notwithstanding this

extinguisher to the entertainments of the evening
Mr. Anderson,—while some are dozing and hob-a-
nobbing in their dreams,—may still be heard keeping
it up with unabated spirit in the dark, wakening every
sleeper now and then with some tremendous chorus
he has contrived to get up among his friends, for the
" Bay of Biscay," or some favourite Greenland
melody, with its inspiriting burthen of " Cheeri-lie,
ah ! cheeri-lie."

Each of us got up, as may be supposed, pretty soon
next morning, and certainly not much refreshed by
our over-night's performances, and after a rough journey over broken ice, arranged to camp early, in order
to give us time before dark to erect a snow-house, and
avoid the black hole of Calcutta style of encampment
of the previous night.   As these snow-houses will
figure somewhat largely in the subsequent part of
this narrative, I may take this opportunity of attempting to give the reader some idea of this novel
species of architecture.   The process of constructing
a snow-house goes on something in this way—varied
of course by circumstances of time, place, and materials.   First, a number of square blocks are cut

PROCESS OF BUILDING A SNOW HOUSE

out of any hard drifted bank of snow you can meet
with, adapted for the purpose, which, when cut (we
generally employed a hand-saw for this), have precisely the appearance of the blocks of salt sold in
the donkey-carts in the streets of London. The dimensions we generally selected were two feet in
length, by fourteen inches in height, and nine inches
in breadth. A layer of these blocks is laid on the
ground nearly in the form of a square, and then
another layer on this, cut so as to incline slightly
inwards, and the corner blocks laid diagonally
over those underneath, so as to cut off the angles.
Other layers follow in the same way, until you have
gradually a dome-shaped structure rising before
you, out of which you have only to cut a small
hole for a door, to find yourself within a very light,
comfortable-looking bee-hive on a large scale, in
which you can bid defiance to wind and weather.
Any chinks between the blocks are filled up with
loose snow with the hand from the outside; as these
are best detected from within, a man is usually sent
in to drive a thin rod through the spot where he dis-
covers a chink, which is immediately plastered over

by some one from without, till the whole house is as
air-tight as an egg.

By this addition to our domestic arrangements we
were able to enjoy a comfortable night's rest, and to
proceed with spirit on our journey the following
morning. In the course of the day we passed the
scene of Mr. Bellot's mishap, which, as already stated,
caused his return to the ship, on the occasion of his
second attempt to reach Whaler Point. As we dug
out of a hard drifted snow bank the various relics of
the disaster—now the remnants of the broken sleigh,
and now a frozen *omnium gatherum* of buffalo robes,
pemmican, beef, biscuit, and dog-traces—we of course
heard the whole story over again; how Mr. John
Smith, seated majestically in his Esquimaux curricle,
and driving his flying coursers over the smooth ice,
with all the pride of a victor in the Olympic Games,
suddenly found himself paddling for dear life in
twenty fathoms water, among barking dogs and
broken fragments of ice. Poor John's recollection
of his cold-bath was nothing to the horrible after-
process of stripping him naked on the ice, until his
companions could muster among them a change of

dry clothing, one supplying a shirt, and another a pair of stockings, a third a great coat, and so on, until our unfortunate Chancellor was once more set upon his legs, and hurried some sixteen miles back to the ship.

We reached the ship next day about 4 P.M., all well and in the highest spirits, and it is hardly necessary to say, received a most cordial welcome from our old shipmates, who, having descried our approach from some distance, came out in a body on the ice to meet us. We had some trouble to satisfy their eager inquiries after each and every individual of the party, they had so long, almost, given over for lost. " Is Kenneth here?" " Where is Gideon Smith?" " Let me see him!" " Where is A, and B, and C?" —might be heard on every side, till one after another, we had all been fairly presented, and our friends, with some difficulty, convinced that we really stood before them in propriâ personâ, and were not merely the disembodied spirits of their departed companions.

With our return to the vessel, may be said to have closed all our operations, as far as the ship was concerned in the Arctic seas for the year 1851. There remained now only to make our arrangements for the vessel passing the next six or eight months where we were, and for preparing for our own winter journeys. The first part of the business was soon completed. The hold was first emptied of some portion of the stores on board, which were laid out on the ice, alongside ; the decks were cleared of lumber, and covered with a housing, extending from near the foremast to the stern, and the whole vessel then embanked with snow as high as the gunwales, leaving only a narrow passage for an entrance, nearly amidships. Outhouses were next built of snow, such as washhouses, a carpenter's shop, a forge, &c. All the powder on board was taken ashore, and secured in a snow-house, out of the reach of fire.

All proper arrangements were, of course, made from the beginning, for securing the health and comfort of the crew and the cleanliness of the vessel, and then came the apportioning of the daily routine of duty for each man on board, for I may as well say at once, that with the extensive winter journeys we contemplated, we could afford no time for the balls, theatrical representations, and other amusements of that nature, which figure so cheerfully and pleasantly in the narratives of the winter occupations of our predecessors. Eight hours were regularly occupied every day in various preparations, connected with the travelling parties, which I saw no good reason to delay sending out, as had heretofore been the practice, till the spring had set in. Some were accordingly employed in making mocassins and winter clothing, others in turning snow-shoe frames and sledges—all in short engaged " quisque pro suo ingenio" in the general work of preparation.

We were indebted to the generous kindness of my esteemed friend, Mr. Barrow, of the Admiralty, for an excellent and well assorted library, supplied to the Prince Albert on her first voyage, and again on this, by means of which, we were enabled to pass our long winter evenings both pleasantly and I trust profitably. We had our Arctic school too, after working hours, superintended by Mr. Cowie, who occasionally enlivened his prelections on the mysteries of the multiplication table, and the curving of " pot-hooks and hangers," by reading aloud, from some work in our library, such extracts as were adapted for the entertainment or instruction of his pupils. Nor did we omit, as the appropriate and befitting conclusion to the labours of each day, to offer up to Him who tempers the wind to the shorn lamb, our heartfelt prayers that we might be guided by His infinite mercy to the accomplishment of the great object in which we were engaged, and be blessed as the instruments of carrying relief to our long-lost brethren.

A few extracts, from my winter journal, will bring up the narrative of our proceedings to the beginning of the year, when, for the first time, the state of the ice in Prince Regent's Inlet, admitted of any extended excursion from the ship, being undertaken with safety.

Tuesday, October 28th.—Mr. Bellot, and a party of four men, left us for the place, (now called Wreck Point), where the sledge had been lost on the 13th inst. in order to bring back as much of the property as could be recovered, and which, in our journey from Whaler Point, we had been unable to bring along with us. The crew set to various employments; some erecting the snow-house to secure the powder on shore, others bringing on board snow and ice, to be melted for a supply of water, and raising an embankment of snow about the mahogany boat.

Wednesday, 29th.—Mr. Bellot and party returned in the afternoon, bringing with them the wreck of the sledge, and other articles for which they had been sent yesterday.   Mr. Bellot reports that the ice, in the Inlet, is now all broken up, and setting south-ward.   We are fortunately moored in a very excel-lent situation, and have no danger to apprehend from this cause.   Batty Bay is unquestionably one of the finest harbours on this coast, being secured from the effects of wind and ice by a shoal on the south side of the entrance to the harbour, and a long spit of land on the north, with a narrow, but deep channel between, in some parts not less than ten fathoms.

Batty Bay, I may mention, was so named by Sir Edward Parry after his friend the late Lieut.-Colonel Batty, who, I learn, served in the Grenadier Guards during the campaign of the Western Pyrenees and at Waterloo, where he was wounded and suffered ever after,—a man of most amiable disposition, and highly gifted mind, and particularly skilled as an artist.

A conspicuous hill, on the north side of the bay, frequently visited by us in the course of the winter, I have named Mount Rosamond, in memory of a favourite daughter of Colonel Batty, prematurely removed from a scene she was in every way calculated to adorn, and who had another claim upon our notice as the grand-daughter of Sir John Barrow.

The weather has been very boisterous for some time past, with heavy showers of snow falling every day. The sun was for a very short time visible today. The Aurora Borealis bright in the south-west about 9 P. M.

Monday, Nov. 10th.—On the suggestion of one of the officers, we have, for some days, been trying an experiment to see how far the exposure of our salt provisions to the frost, and burying them in the snow, would have the effect of freshening (that is, drawing out the salt from) them : but we have had no reason to put any faith in it. We have been endeavouring, also, to add to our fresh stock, in another and more effectual way. For the last fortnight, much of the leisure time of the officers has been devoted to hunting excursions in the neighbourhood, but this locality appears to be unusually destitute of animal life. Occasionally as many as ten ptarmigan have been bagged in a day : but this is rare good fortune. Some foxes have been trapped also, though very rarely, and some of us have enjoyed the delicacy of a fox-pie, which has been pronounced by competent authorities in our mess to be equal to rabbit; but with the impartiality of an historian, I am bound to admit there are others to whom it suggests uncomfortable reminiscences of dead cats, and who generally, therefore, prefer the opposite side of the table, whenever it makes its appearance. A stray Polar-bear or two, and a solitary raven, make up the circle of our Zoologial acquaintance in Batty Bay.

Mr. Bellot makes daily pilgrimages to a hill in the neighbourhood, where he occasionally succeeds in getting a meridian observation of the sun, and *always* succeeds in getting his fingers frozen in the operation.

My own time is almost wholly taken up in superintending the preparations for the winter journeys. Very few on board have ever seen a snow-shoe, or a dog-sleigh before, and none of them know how they

are constructed, John Smith excepted, and even he
is not altogether *au fait* in some essential details. I
am at present deep in a course of lectures, " with
experiments and illustrations," as our scientific friends
in London would say, on the art and mystery of
cutting "babiche," lacing snow-shoes, steaming and
piercing tough boards of beech for sleighs, making
harness for dogs, &c. We have turned out already
a very respectable pair of snow-shoes, which the
reader will have a very good idea of, if he can imagine
a cane-bottomed rout-seat, about five feet long, with
the legs sawed off, each end tapering to a point, and
the toe end curved up about five inches from the
frame. A lacing or net-work of thin thongs of
parchment about the thickness of whip-cord (termed
by the initiated " babiche,") takes the place of the
cane-bottom in our illustration. You have only now
to strengthen your frame-work by transverse bars of
wood, about an inch square, and six or eight inches
apart; plant your foot in the middle—fasten your
shoe on as you would a pair of pattens or a pair of
skates, and you are ready to march

" Over the hills and far away ;

over endless abysses of snow, where you might often
be left to flounder, were you not provided with this
most useful and indeed indispensable foot gear for
travellers in the Arctic regions.

Monday, 1*st Dec.*—Our reconnoitring parties report that the ice, though still drifting southward in
the body of the Inlet, begins to set along shore; since
the last date there has been a continuance of westerly
gales, accompanied with heavy falls of snow.   The
general routine of the duties of the men continues
the same, and we are making visible progress in the
all-absorbing preparations for the travelling parties.
Our short daily excursions from the ship are furnishing us with much useful experience in a variety of
ways, which we trust to be able to turn to account in
our future operations.   Woollen clothes of all kinds
we find are not well adapted for travelling, from their
imbibing so much of the fine snow drift; and to
obviate this, as far as possible, I have given directions to have all the clothing intended for the winter
journey covered with cotton, which we find renders
it almost impervious to the snow.

Our apparatus, again, for cooking by the flame of

spirits of wine, termed a " conjuror" (for what reason 'twould puzzle one to say), is so complicated by a mechanism of screws and burners, requiring to be adjusted by the naked hand, that we have been under the necessity of substituting (what we have certainly found a great improvement on this part of the apparatus), an open hexagonal-shaped dish, with grooves at the covers for the wicks. An equable and continuous flame is thus produced without the neccessity of exposing the naked hand to the contact of cold metal.

Monday, 8th.—I have observed that the wind which has continued westerly for a long period, is gradually veering towards the north, and generally speaking, within the last few days, very variable. John and Gideon Smith, while taking a walk yesterday, found a white fox evidently killed by the dogs. However strange, it nevertheless appears correct, that although Esquimaux dogs may kill a fox, they will not eat him. This is the more extraordinary, as they are in the estimation of our worthy doctor the most voracious and dirty-feeding animals he ever knew. Nothing they can possibly get at

being safe.   Buffalo robes, seal-skins, their own harness, even boots, shoes, clothes and dish-cloths, being
sure to be destroyed.

Monday, 22nd Dec., shortest day.—Fine mild
agreeable weather, with fine light W.N.W. airs
throughout.   Shortest day hailed with pleasure, for
although time cannot as yet be said, with our constant
occupation, to hang heavy on our hands, yet we shall
now gladly count the days that must elapse before
we may expect the return of the sun.

Thursday, 25th, Christmas-day.—A very fine,
calm, mild day throughout.   It passed off very
quietly, in a manner indeed that our friends in England would, I fear, consider decidedly flat.   Great
preparations had been made for a shooting match to
celebrate the day; but the darkness was so great,
that to avoid the risk of shooting each other, the
match had to be put off.   A game at foot-ball was
accordingly substituted.   Music and cards, and such
extra good cheer as our stores afforded, helped to
enliven the day, and we closed it with what I fear
were some very dull speeches from the Commander
downwards, upon the cardinal virtues expected

to be displayed by all, after the next week or fortnight, when, as it was now finally determined, the long-talked of winter journeys were to commence.

CHAPTER IV.

WINTER JOURNEY TO FURY BEACH.

Monday, Jan. 5th, 1852—WAS ushered in by that heterogeneous collection of sounds, familiar to the ear of the Arctic voyager, as the prelude to a winter journey in these regions—a general clatter of snow-shoes and dog-sleighs, a cracking of whips, and a snarling and howling of dogs, mad with torment and impatience.

The crew of the "Prince Albert," were all on the

ice, but it was evident that they were not all destined for the journey. Any eye might pick out the five travellers; viz. Mr. Bellot, myself, John Smith, W. Millar, and W. Adamson. Dressed out in our travelling costume, we presented, I have no doubt, a somewhat singular and original appearance—every man with his clothing coated with cotton, some white, some black, and others striped, looking for all the world as if some mischievous Puck, had turned every article of dress outside in, before it had been put on.

The first object of the contemplated journey was of course to ascertain whether Fury Beach had been a retreating point to any of Sir John Franklin's party since it was visited by Lieut. Robinson of the Enterprise in 1849. A secondary object, should our expectations in this respect not be realized, was to form a first depôt of provisions here, with the view of carrying out a more extended search as soon as circumstances would permit.

It was desirable at the same time to ascertain the state of the *roads*, by which of course I mean the yet untrodden surface of the snow or ice, in the direction in which we meant to go, before commencing any transport on a large scale between the ship and Fury Beach, and it was thought advisable therefore on this occasion to go comparatively light. A small supply of pemmican was therefore all we took with us in addition to our travelling requirements, consisting of a tent and poles, blanketing and provisions for a week, some guns and ammunition, fuel, and cooking apparatus, in all weighing from 200 to 250 lbs. This, with ordinary roads, was what four dogs, now with us, could draw on a flat native sleigh, with the utmost ease; but on such ground as that we soon met with, on rounding the south head-land of Batty Bay, to which we were escorted by Messrs. Leask and Cowie, and a part of the crew, we soon found that we required the united efforts of both men and dogs to get along at all, and accordingly for the rest of the journey we pulled together in the most amicable and fraternal style imaginable.

The ice on the inlet being still detached from the shore, and moving bodily towards the south, no other path was left us to follow than that along the base of the lofty cliffs, that extend in an almost unbroken line from Batty Bay to within three miles of Fury

Beach. This, as may readily be imagined, was by no means a very easy road to follow. Obstructions beset us at every step, which it required often the utmost exertion of our motley and heterogeneous company of men and dogs to surmount.

The path was covered with boulders and fragments of ice, stranded on the beach by some former tempest, which made the dragging of the sleigh amongst them a much more difficult and laborious operation than if the whole weight had been divided and carried upon our shoulders. Sometimes too what is called a "pressure," or a set of the ice upon the shore, would be found to have blocked up the way altogether, and in such cases, our only resource was to cut a passage through with the axe. The most common form of obstacle, however, arose from the numerous sloping banks of hard drifted snow piled up against the face of the cliffs, and leaving us only a steep inclined plane to scramble over as we best could with the dogs and sleigh. These troublesome inclines we generally contrived, after a great expenditure of time and labour, to get over without any accident, but not unfrequently after toiling to the top, a lurch

of the sleigh would send us careering in a very lively
and unexpected manner to the bottom. Here follows
an incident in our first day's journey, which caused
us some amusement at the time, and carried a lesson
with it, whenever we had to encounter any of these
obstacles afterwards.

We had got about half-way up one of those
villanous steeps, when our entire cortege gave unmis-
takeable signs of a tendency to seek a sudden descent.
There was just time for us to cast off the traces, all
but poor Mr. Bellot, who was not sufficiently alert
in disengaging his, when away went the sleigh and
dogs, and Mr. Bellot after them, into an abyss at the
bottom, where the only indication of the catastrophe
that could be seen was some six inches of Mr.
Bellot's heels above the surface of the snow. We dug
him out "a wiser and a better man" for the rest of
the journey, whenever any of these pestilent slopes
had to be encountered thereafter.

The sun had disappeared at the ship on the 30th
Oct., and owing to the position of some high hills to
the south of us, did not re-appear before the 15th of
Feb. ; it was therefore entirely by moon-light that we

H

were enabled to travel at all, and on an obscure night
we might rather be said to be groping our way through
the obstacles that beset us, in darkness that made
itself be felt, than travelling after any recognized
fashion known to men, even in the Arctic regions.
Owing to the various obstructions now mentioned,
we did not make more than ten miles from the ship
during our first day's journey, when the darkness
compelled us to encamp, and it being too late to con-
struct a snow-house, we were forced to take shelter
for the night under the tent, which we endeavoured
to make as comfortable as we could by embanking
the bottom with snow.   The dogs were left without
to shift for themselves as they best could, and
provided they had a sufficient supply of food, we
found that their strength and vigour were the reverse
of impaired by their bivouac in the snow.

  Tuesday, 6th.—About six A.M., after breakfasting
on tea, pemmican, and biscuit, our travelling fare
during this, as well as all our other journeys, we resumed our course, struggling with precisely the same
difficulties as those we had to encounter yesterday.   In
the course of the day we fell upon two old tent encamp-

ments, probably those of the retreating party of Sir John Ross in 1833; but, beyond this, found no indications of this part of the coast having ever been visited by any foot or boat party. After travelling about eight hours, we put up for the night at the foot of a high precipice, with a perpendicular mass of stranded ice at the bottom, which served for the gable end of a snow-house we erected against it, and in which we reposed for the night, with a far higher degree of comfort than we had been able to obtain the night before from the tent. During the night we were honoured with an Arctic serenade, in the form of a " pressure," from the moving ice, which, after grinding and groaning, anything but mellifluously in our ears all night, more like "noises in a swound," left us in the morning with a pile of fragments of ice at least thirty feet in height, within twenty yards of our encampment.

Wednesday, 7th.—Fell upon more traces of Sir John Ross's party, consisting of three cases of preserved vegetable soup, still in excellent condition, a small quantity of coal and wood, and some iron hoops, apparently of a biscuit-cask.

We had some heavy work with the axe through the rough hummocky ice, and more difficult travelling altogether than we had yet experienced. After fighting our way through a host of our old enemies, the snow-banks, we were about three P.M. brought to a dead halt, by a perpendicular cliff overhanging a mass of moving ice, which swept up to its very base along the shore. While the rest of the party were engaged in constructing a snow-house at the point where we had been arrested, further progress that day being out of the question, I succeeded in getting to the top of the cliff by cutting steps with the axe as I ascended, my object being to obtain a view of the coast as well as of Fury Beach, and to ascertain whether the remainder of the journey might not be better effected by land. The result of this survey was a determination to leave our sleigh and baggage in charge of two of the men where we were, and proceed with the rest to Fury Beach early next morning.

Thursday, 8th.—In pursuance of the resolution come to yesterday, Mr. Bellot, John Smith, and myself, set out at an early hour for Fury Beach, with a

determination to reach it that night. Being now
unencumbered with the sleigh, we got over the
ground much more rapidly than we had hitherto
done, and towards five o'clock found ourselves within
sight of it.

We had already in our eagerness, aided by the
marvellously refractive powers of an Arctic haze, mistaken, to our no small amusement, when we discovered it, a stranded packing-case, that lay on the
beach on our way, for Sir John Ross's Somerset
House, and on another occasion had well nigh found
our way to the bottom of a precipice, that suddenly
yawned beneath our feet, as we marched on absorbed
in the exciting feelings of the moment, and utterly
regardless of the sublunary consideration of looking
where we were going. But for Mr. Bellot's presence
of mind, and the keener vision of his younger eyes,
I verily believe that he and myself would then and
there have ended our mortal career.

It may be imagined with what feelings, when we
really had come upon it, we approached a spot round
which so many hopes and anxieties had so long cen-
tered. Every object, distinguished by the moonlight

in the distance became animated to our imaginations,
into the forms of our long-absent countrymen; for
had they been imprisoned anywhere in the Arctic
seas, within a reasonable distance of Fury Beach,
here we felt assured some of them at least would
have been now. But alas! for these fond hopes!
how deeply, though perhaps unconsciously cherished,
none of us probably suspected, till standing under the
tattered covering of Somerset House and gazing
silently upon the solitude around us, we felt as we
turned to look mournfully on each other's faces that
the last ray of hope, as to this cherished imagination,
had fled from our hearts.   It is perhaps necessary for
the vigorous prosecution of any difficult object that for
the moment, some particular circumstance in the
chain of operations by which it is to be effected
should seem to us so vitally important that the eye
is blinded to all beyond.   The spot on which we
now stood had so long been associated in our minds
with some clue to the discovery of the solution of
the painful mystery which hung over the fate of
Franklin, and had so long unconsciously perhaps
coloured all our thoughts, that it was not without a

pang, and a feeling as if the main purpose of our
expedition had been defeated, that we found all our
long cherished anticipations shattered at a blow by
the scene which met our eyes. Thus my friend and
I stood paralyzed at the death-like solitude around us.
No vestige of the visit of a human being was here
since Lieut. Robinson had examined the depôt in
1849. The stores, still in the most perfect preservation, were precisely in the well arranged condition,
described in the clear report of that energetic
officer.

His own notice of his visit was deeply buried in the
snow, and the index staff he had placed over it was
thrown down and gnawed by the foxes. Wearied
with a long and fruitless examination we took up
our quarters for a repose of a few hours in Somerset
House, the frame of which was still standing entire,
but the covering blown to rags by the wind, and one
end of the house nearly filled with snow. We lighted
a fire on the stove which had heated the end occupied
by Sir John Ross's crew during the dreary winter of
1832-33.

After refreshing ourselves with a warm supper,

and nodding for a few hours over the fire, we set out
about 11 P.M. on our return to our encampment,
which we reached by 2 A.M. of the following morning.
Our return from this point to the ship, which we
reached about 5 P.M. of Saturday the 10th, was not
marked by any incident worthy of notice. We had
deposited at our encampment a 90 lbs. case of pemmican, a bag of coals, two muskets, and some ammunition, which while it served as a reserve for future
explorations in this direction, materially lightened the
labour of the dogs, and allowed us time for a more
minute examination of the coast than we had been
able to make during the outward journey. The
result, however, was not in any respect more successful. No traces of any kind were discovered which
could throw light on the objects of our search.

As a fact in natural history, it may be interesting
to some to state that during our return we met with
two ravens on the site of one of Sir John Ross's old
encampments—the solitary denizens of these wastes
during the cheerless gloom of an Arctic winter. We
met with no other living creatures; hardly even a
trace of their existence to break the universal and

awful solitude which appears to reign over these
regions during the depth of mid-winter.

Thus ended our first journey to Fury Beach, and
its result satisfied us, that in the present state of
the ice in Prince Regent's Inlet, the more extended
exploration of the coast line, which we had calculated
on being able to commence on our return to the
ship, could not now be safely undertaken, and must
for the present be postponed. We were most reluctantly compelled therefore to pass the next month in
the ship, occupied in the same general routine duties
as those on which we had been engaged during the
earlier part of the winter.

Whether from any unusual mildness of the season,
or from other causes, I cannot undertake to decide,
but I was much struck by the fact that the cold
experienced by us during the months of January and
February was not by several degrees so intense as I
had observed in other parts of the continent of North
America in much lower latitudes. On one occasion
the thermometer descended to 48°, but the average
indication for the coldest months of winter was not
much below 30°. Comparing this with the meteorological observations of Sir John Ross in 1833, one of

two conclusions seems inevitable, either that the cold decreases in these latitudes with the progress northward, or that the winter of 1851-52 was an unusually mild one.

The terrible enemies of our travelling parties were the snow-storms and the furious gales which prevailed with us during the greater part of the winter. A low temperature, even the lowest recorded in the Arctic regions, is elysium compared with a piercing nor'-easter driving the sharp keen spiculæ of snow-drift, like a shower of red-hot sand in your face and through every pore of your body. The comparison may seem Hibernian, but nevertheless gives a very good idea of one's sensations under the pitiless dis-charge of a hurricane of snow-drift in these regions, where as in Milton's Pandemonium,

————" The parched air
Burns frore, and cold performs the effect of fire."

I have a strong opinion that old Æolus, with his den of ruffianly winds, that so shamefully belaboured the pious Æneas, must have emigrated to North Somerset since the days of Virgil. Such a high carnival of northerly gales as, during the winter months, swept round the poor little Albert, and nearly smothered

us under an avalanche of snow, I believe never was
heard of in any other known region of the globe.
Where they all came from, and how they did not long
before the winter was over blow themselves fairly
out, was a wonder to us all the year round. "I have
known but one gale since we entered Batty Bay,"
once observed our veteran friend Hepburn, "and that
was the gale that began when we came and ended
when we went away." It was of no use going out of a
morning on the strength of an hour's lull in the
elemental war, and trusting to have a quiet view of
the ice in the inlet, or a shot at a bear, or a run
after a fox ; as surely as you had got a mile from the
ship, and were congratulating yourself on a good
bracing hour or two's exercise, you would be caught
in a swirling deluge of drift, through which it was impossible to see your way six paces off. Of one of these
excursions some of us in the Prince Albert have very
substantial reasons for retaining a very lively recollection to this day.

About eight A.M in the morning of the 13th
February, Mr. Bellot, the carpenter, Andrew
Irvine, Henry Anderson (the first mate), and myself,

left the ship, taking with us two cases of pemmican
and three tin jars, each containing two gallons of
spirits of wine, on a sledge, drawn by five Esquimaux
dogs, for the purpose of depositing them a short distance on the way to Fury Beach, and returning in
the evening.   After proceeding for a few hours, and
making very fair progress along a tolerably good
path, a strong wind arose, which by one P.M. had
increased to a perfect hurricane, so thickly charged
with snow that, in attempting to cross a bay on our
return, we lost sight of the land by which our course
homeward had been guided.   In short, after wandering about for some time, scarcely able to distinguish each other at the distance of a few paces,
we found that we had fairly lost our way.   In this
dilemma, we set two of the five dogs loose from the
sledge, in the hope that they would act as guides better
than when drawing ; but this proved to be a mistake,
as they would not leave the others.   At last, however,
they all set off together, taking the sledge with them,
and leaving us to our fate.   As we afterwards found,
they reached the ship without any difficulty, and, as
may readily be supposed, put every one on board in

a perfect fever of terror and anxiety as to what had become of us. In the meantime we had gone on floundering over the broken ice, until we had once more stumbled on the land, but where or what the land was we had fallen upon, nobody knew. It was something certainly, to know we were not marching over the Inlet or out to sea, in which case we would have marched on, and in all probability never returned; but in other respects we had rather lost than gained by getting on terra-firma. With an atmosphere as thick as pea-soup, and no sun, moon, or stars to be seen, there was no keeping the shore (and to go on one side or the other was to incur the certainty of losing ourselves again, either on the Inlet or on the land), without hugging close up and into a breakneck line of stranded fragments of ice, which indicated the direction of the beach. Along this formidable path we floundered on—now coming bump up against some huge fragment of ice, or pitching over the top of it into a hole, excavated in the snow at the bottom, by the whirling eddies of the wind; now walking, now crawling, occasionally tumbling into the snow, until we were all suddenly brought up by a cry of pain from one of the men, who had met with a *bouleversement* over the edge of a bank of ice. It was a sad accident, but the worst of it was, that after setting him on his legs, nothing could induce him to move a step farther. Here he was, and here he maintained he must remain " *coute qui coute.*" There was no reasoning with the poor fellow, who certainly had sustained a very severe injury, but not anything like so bad as he had imagined it, and it would never do to leave him lying here. So feigning to take him at his word, we proposed to bundle him up in a buffalo-robe and bury him in the snow for the night—comforting him with the assurance that we would certainly come back for him in the morning.

This Arctic prescription had a magical effect upon our patient—the back and the broken bones were speedily forgotten, and in a short time he was on his legs again, and we all trudging on once more in the old rough and tumble style of progression, till about midnight, we found ourselves standing under the lee of something which looked like a bank of snow, but which, to our great gratification, proved to be the powder-house we had erected on shore in the beginning of the winter. A consultation was now held whether we should cut our way into it and pass the night here, " accoutred as we were," or make for the ship, which we now knew could not be far off. Our decision was for the latter, and the only question now was, how to steer for the vessel. This, too, was decided upon at last, by each of the party pointing in turn in the direction in which he thought the vessel lay, and then taking the mean of the bearings. To prevent our separating in the drift (for some of the party had by this time got so benumbed with cold, as to be unable to use their hands to clear their eyelids, and had thus become literally blind with the accumulation of the snow on their eyes), it was agreed that at certain intervals we should call and answer to each other's names, and that those whose eyes had suffered least should take the others in tow. In this order we proceeded for the vessel, and fortunately by the guidance of a solitary star, that could be faintly distinguished through the drift, got near enough the ship to hear the wind whistling through the shrouds, and were thus guided, rather by the ear than by the eye, to her position, and soon afterwards found ourselves on board, where we were received once more as those from the dead.

It is hardly necessary to say that we were all dreadfully frost-bitten. With such precautions, however, as we took, carefully restoring the circulation of the affected parts by rubbing them over with cold water and snow, *before* going below, we escaped with no worse consequences than some very ugly-looking scars, and two or three days of snow-blindness, with, of course, the doctor's best attention for the first fortnight thereafter.

Amidst such incidents as these, relieving the monotony of ship duties, and varied by an occasional bear-hunt, or a chase after a fox, the months of January and February wore on, till, towards the end of the latter month, our preparations for the long contemplated " grand journey" were completed. This journey, as it forms the leading feature of our Expedition, and was, indeed, the main object in view on our leaving England, will require a fuller detail than within the limits to which I have restricted myself in this little book, I could afford to our proceedings up to this date. The particular direction our route ought to assume, was of course a matter to be regulated very much by the nature of the circumstances that might arise in the course of it. On one point only we were decided—viz. that it should embrace Cape Walker, to which, as the point of departure of Sir John Franklin for the unknown regions to the W. and S.W., had he decided upon this course, and not gone up Wellington Channel, much interest naturally attached.

There were fourteen of the crew disposable in the ship, of whom four picked men were to go with Mr. Bellot and myself to Cape Walker, while the rest were to accompany us, as a fatigue party, as far as Fury Beach, which was to form the starting point of the journey. Parties sent out on different occasions during the last two months, had taken in advance six cases of pemmican, six muskets and a bag of coals. One case of pemmican, as already mentioned, had been deposited in January a few miles north of Fury Point. Our provisions, clothing, and bedding, drawn upon two Indian sleighs by our five dogs, had, of course, been reduced to whatever was strictly indispensable. Five gallons of spirits of wine were taken as a substitute for fuel. With proper management and economy, we hoped to make this last us till the spring, when, by the plan we proposed adopting, of travelling during the night instead of the day, we trusted, should a necessity arise for so doing, to be able to dispense with the use of fuel altogether.

On the morning of the 25th of February, a scene of general bustle and excitement shewed that all our arrangements had been completed, and that the long deferred start for the grand journey was about to take place. A detachment of five men, Mr. Bellot, and myself, were all that could leave the ship at this time; the others appointed to join us being still under the Doctor's attendance for slight and temporary inconvenience, frost bites, &c. The whole crew however had mustered to see us as far as the south point of Batty Bay, all but our dear Hepburn, who unable to control his manly emotion at parting with so many old friends, and above all at being unable to accompany us, took a touching farewell of us at the vessel : " God bless you," said he, grasping my hand with affectionate warmth, " I cannot accompany you, and I cannot let all these men witness my emotion: let me part with you here, and may God grant that we meet again in life and health, after the long and hazardous journey you are about to undertake." Though this veteran hero saw much hardship and hazard in store before us, he would have seen none whatever had he been allowed to accompany us, but I could not for a moment entertain the idea of employing him on a journey, when there were so many younger men all emulous to be engaged on it, and more particularly when his services on board ship were so indispensable; and, by his kindly consenting to remain, I was relieved of all anxiety as respected the Prince Albert.

Reaching the south point of Batty Bay, with our friendly escort, our two parties once more separated with many kindly and touching farewells, and then with three hearty cheers, diverging in our different routes, we were soon lost to each other in the mist and snow.

The incidents of the first stage of our journey up to Fury Beach, need not be particularly described, as the reader has already been conducted over this part of the route during our first excursion. Mr. Bellot accompanied us only for the first day, and was then instructed to return alone to the ship, and bring up a reinforcement of men and stores, as early as it might be found practicable to join us at this point. Owing to the violence of the equinoctial gales prevalent at this season, which kept us a whole week on one occasion detained in an encampment, I did not reach Fury Beach with the remaining five men before the 5th of March.

Of our "experiences" during our week's detention at our encampment, I find the following notices in the rough notes of my journal.

The gale of Saturday (28th February), continuing during three days, we were of necessity compelled to remain in camp. During a short interval on the 2nd of March, the weather appearing to get more moderate, we were enabled to return for what cargo had been left behind during our former trip. It was taken onward as far as we dared, and we returned to the camp against a wind so keen that no face escaped being frost bitten—the strong wind in this instance being the cause, rather than the degree of temperature,

for this was comparatively moderate. On the morning
of the 3rd a lull of an hour or so, enticed us to bundle
up and lash our sleigh. No sooner, had we done
this and proceeded a short distance than the gale
came on with redoubled fury ; in consequence of
which we had to hasten back to our snow retreat,
and were glad enough to have been still so near a
shelter when caught by it, as we had much difficulty in
keeping on our feet from the violence of the whirling
eddies, that came sweeping along an exposed headland
near us. Such was the force of the wind, that
column after column of whirling spray was raised by
it out of a continuous lane of water, more than a mile
broad, which the present gale had opened out along
the coast, at the distance of only a few yards from
our present encampment. As these successive columns
were lifted out of the water, they were borne
onward with a speed scarcely less rapid than the
" wings of the wind " itself. Whilst detained here
we narrowly escaped being buried by an *infant*
avalanche. A hardened mass of snow of several tons
in weight having been disengaged from the summit
of the cliff above us, by the sweeping winds, came

rolling down with a noise that told fearfully of its approach. In its descent it carried along with it several fragments of rock that lay in its path, and at length, being able to advance no farther, lodged itself within a few yards of our present dwelling, after ploughing up a bed for itself in the hard packed snow before it, and doing us no other harm than scattering a few harmless masses of snow about the base of our encampment, which brought forth the words from one of our party, " Come, boys, let us run,"—to the no small merriment of the rest.

Since the commencement of this gale the entire sheet of ice on Regent's Inlet, as far as it could be seen, was noticed to be in a state of motion to the southward; how this may be accounted for I am at a loss to say, unless on the supposition that a vast number of " pressures " were taking place in the southern portion of the Inlet, and thus making room for the large quantity of ice that was invariably seen going south.

On the 7th March, Mr. Bellot joined us at Fury Beach with seven men, making in all fourteen now collected at this spot.

Such was the state of the ground between the ship
and this point, added to the violence of the weather,
and the obstructions arising from the numerous
lanes of open water along the shore, sometimes two
miles in breadth, that this short distance made greater
havoc in our equipment than all the rest of the subsequent journey put together. The damage to the
sleighs, snow-shoes and canvas mocassins, was so
great, that we had in fact to begin our preparations
anew, and send a party of eight men back to the ship
for fresh supplies, before we could undertake to
continue the journey.

We had helped ourselves very liberally from the
old stores of the Fury, which we found not only
in the best preservation, but much superior in quality,
after thirty years of exposure to the weather, to some
of our own stores, and those supplied to the other
Arctic Expeditions. This high state of preservation,
I cannot help attributing in some measure to the
strength and thickness of the tins, in which the
preserved meats, vegetables, and soups had been
placed. The flour had all caked in solid lumps,
which had to be re-ground and passed through a sieve

before it was fit for the cook's hands. In other respects it was fresh and sweet as ever, and supplied us with a stock of excellent biscuit.

Owing to these various causes of detention, it was the 29th of March before we were able finally to set out upon our march southward. As we now enter upon new ground I shall in future give the daily incidents of our route from the rough notes of my journal.

CHAPTER V.

THE LONG JOURNEY.

AFTER the various accidents and detentions which
had delayed our journey up to this period, we were

heartily glad to be able at 9 A.M. of the 29th March, to take our final departure from Fury Beach. It had been arranged that our whole party, consisting as already stated of fourteen men, should proceed together as far as Brentford Bay, whence eight were to be sent back to the ship, while the remaining six proceeded on the journey. Our object in this arrangement will be readily understood. To husband the resources of the long party, who had probably three months of travelling before them, and upwards of a thousand miles to get over in that time, was obviously an object of the utmost importance. The supply of provisions which six men could carry along with them, would be utterly inadequate to the performance of so long a journey, but by making Brentford Bay our starting point, and bringing the relief party thus far with us, the consumption for that distance at any rate would be saved.

Our equipments from Fury Beach, upon which so much of the success of our undertaking depended, were as follows.

lbs.

8⅓ cases of pemmican, each 90lb. weighing
    in all   750

4 bags of biscuits, each 75lb.   .   .   300

1 small sack of flour   .   .   .   30

3 small bags of coal, each 40lbs. .   .   120

Several bundles of firewood, about   .   112

3 tin cases of spirits of wine, say 5 gallons   25

A case of ammunition, knives, files, hooks,
    &c. intended for the Esquimaux, weighing
    about   60

1 bag containing our astronomical instru-
    ments, books, &c.   .   .   .   30

Several bags containing our bedding, sugar,
    and tea, guns, axes, saws, cutlasses, kettles,
    pots and pans, weighing in all not less
    than   200

Total weight, about   .   .   .   1627

If to this be added the weight of the sledges and
tackling, the total dead weight of our equipments
might be estimated at about 2000lbs. The whole
was lashed down, to the smallest possible compass,

on four flat-bottomed Indian sleighs, of which our
five Esquimaux dogs, assisted by two men to each
sleigh, took two, while the rest of the men took the
other two.

The weather for this season of the year was
unusually mild, the thermometer rising as high as
—12 at noon.   The land as we proceeded from Fury
Beach became lower and lower, and in many places
was indicated only by a few black spots appearing
through the surface of the snow.   After travelling
six miles, we came to a flat point, where the beach
was found a little broader, with a fine smooth floe
along the shore, affording a good track for the
sleighs.

At 7 P.M., having walked from sixteen to eighteen
geographical miles, we halted for the night, and set
about the preparations for our encampment.   This
was the first time, since the memorable trip from
Whaler Point to the ship, that we had had so large
a party to accommodate for the night, and it was soon
seen that one snow-house could not contain us all.
So it was decided to build two, and to save trouble
they were to be built end to end, with a party wall

between—John Smith and myself acting as chief architects in each division. The lower tiers of the rival buildings were run up in famous style, and we had a neck and neck race of it, till the important process of arching the roof began, when that fatal party wall became a bone of contention, each party maintaining that they were crimped of their fair proportion of support for the arch. In the midst of a hot argument on this point down came one of the houses, amidst a general execration of the Smithites. A second time it was run up and a second time it came down, and before it was at last finished, and we were all in bed, it was past midnight.

30th.—A keen frosty morning, which followed our late repose of last night, found us marching on for Cape Garry, over a succession of level floes and low-lying points, with some striking and original additions to our travelling costume since yesterday. We had all been exercising our ingenuity in the contrivance of various little arrangements for the protection of the face against the effects of the frost, and this morning a curious observer might have studied with some interest the idiosyncracies of indi-

vidual genius as exhibited in the variety of grotesque
appendages to noses, cheeks, eyes, chins, and every
vulnerable spot of the human face divine. For the
eyes we had goggles of glass, of wire-gauze, of crape,
or of plain wood with a slit in the centre, in the
manner of the Esquimaux. For the face some had
cloth masks, with neat little crevices for the mouth,
nose, and eyes; others were muffled up in the ordinary chin-cloth, and for that most troublesome of the
facial members, the nose, (which I verily believe was
made only to be frozen), a strong party, with our
always original carpenter at their head, had gutta-
percha noses, lined with delicate soft flannel, which
warmed one's heart to look at. What powers of
cold could penetrate such a rampart as this? Frost-
bites? pooh! Who fears to encounter anything
and everything in the armoury of King Frost, behind
such seven-fold shields as these?

But alas! for the vanity of human wisdom. The
masks were found in a few hours to be completely
coated with rime, from the congelation of the breath,
and the warm air from the face, and were forthwith
discarded as a nuisance. The gutta-percha nose from

the same cause stuck fast to the skin, which it pulled away with it whenever it required to be unshipped, and forthwith it shared the fate of the masks. The chin-cloths and the goggles held their ground to the last, and did yeoman's service throughout the journey.

While on the subject of these little personal arrangements, I may as well take the opportunity of attempting to give the reader some idea of the routine of our day's march.

At six o'clock, generally (although from various circumstances this hour was not always strictly adhered to), all hands were roused by myself, and the preparations for the march began. Breakfast was the first operation, and then came the bundling up of the bedding, cooking utensils, &c., the lashing of the sleighs, aud the harnessing of the dogs, which, altogether on an average, occupied the next two hours. Then came the start, I leading the way, and selecting the best track for the sleighs, and Mr. Bellot, with the rest of the party, following in regular line with the four sledges. At the end of every hour five minutes were allowed for resting the men and breathing the dogs. When the weather permitted, sights for the chronometer were taken at any convenient hour in the forenoon, and again for latitude, at noon. The proper corrections had been prepared the previous night or morning, so as to enable the observation to be worked off on the spot, without the trouble of referring to books. Half an hour on each occasion generally sufficed to get through all the necessary operations for ascertaining our latitude, or longitude, as the case might be. The construction of the snow-house and the preparations for the evening meal and our repose for the night, concluded the labours of the day, which were seldom over before nine or ten at night.

Thursday, 1st April.—Made the south shore of Cresswell Bay in the afternoon, in thick snowy weather, about five or six miles to the W. of Cape Garry. In the evening we encamped on the point we supposed to be Cape Garry, the land being very low, and no conspicuous head-land in sight, deserving the name of a cape. Numerous tracks of rein-deer and musk oxen were observed immediately on making the shore, in general going northward.

During this and the three following days, we continued our route, without any incident worthy of notice, along a similar low-lying country to that we had hitherto passed; the tracks of rein-deer, wolves, musk-oxen, and bears continuing to increase as we proceeded southward.

Monday, 5*th.*—We were now approaching Brentford Bay, a point of much interest in our route. After passing in the forenoon the remains of a dozen Esquimaux huts, with their usual accompaniment of bones, we halted at noon (the day being unusually clear), to get a meridian altitude, which gave Lat. 72° 01′ 37″ N., var. 140 W. Shortly afterwards we arrived at a rising ground, from which Brentford Bay with its numerous islands, could be distinctly seen and recognized from Sir John Ross's description. About three P.M. we came to the entrance of the bay, and on rounding the north point, struck for a conspicuous island a few miles within the entrance (Brown's Island of Sir John Ross), beyond which a dense column of vapour was issuing apparently from some open channel of water. Camped on the north side of the island at six P.M. At dusk

K

a bear came quite close to our snow-house, and was chased away by the dogs.

Tuesday, 6th.—At eight A.M. the fatigue party who had accompanied us thus far left us to return to the ship; Andrew Irvine, John Smith, Richard Webb, and Wm. Adamson, remaining with Mr. Bellot and myself to continue the journey, as had been previously arranged. By the return party I sent instructions to those in charge at the ship, to forward more provisions to Fury Beach, and if possible to have Mr. Cowie examine Cresswell Bay, with the view of ascertaining whether there was any passage leading out of it to the westward.

The remainder of the day was devoted to the examination of Brentford Bay in two parties. Mr. Bellot and John Smith going southward, and Adamson and myself northward, in the direction of the column of vapour observed yesterday. On coming up to it, we found it to issue from a space of open water, extending for upwards of a mile along a channel leading westward, that might have an average breadth of about two miles. About four miles farther up, a second piece of open water was discovered with pieces of loose ice floating through it, carried up and down by the tide. From a high hill in the neighbourhood, I could plainly distinguish a sea stretching westward, to an estimated distance of about thirty miles, with the channel through which we had come so far, apparently leading into it. Other passages, or what seemed to be passages, were also observed running amongst the hills to the southward, but I was unable to trace their connexion, or to satisfy myself whether they were in reality channels or inlets; on arriving at the encampment we found Mr. Bellot and John Smith returned, who reported having likewise discovered a passage leading westward.

Wednesday, 7th.—Started early, and took the northern channel, partly explored by myself yesterday, and continued along it until six P.M. when we reached its western extremity, a distance of not less than twenty miles, including its various windings. From a high hill near our encampment at this spot, we observed a broad channel running N.N.E. and S.S.W., true (variation 140), which was at first taken for a continuation of Brentford Bay, until its great extent convinced us that we had fallen upon

a western sea or channel, and that the passage we
had just gone through was in reality a strait, leading
out of Prince Regent Inlet.   It appears on the map
of our discoveries as Bellot Strait—a just tribute to
the important services rendered to our Expedition
by Lieutenant Bellot. The island which forms
its southern shore was named Levesque Island,
in accordance with the wishes of Lady Franklin, expressed to me before my departure, that I should
name some place in honour of this esteemed friend
and generous supporter of the original Prince Albert's
Expedition.   The Western Sea, into which the channel opens, we have ascertained since our return to be
the northern extremity of Victoria Strait, partially
explored by Dr. Rae, from another direction. The
hill on which we stood was probably a portion of the
high land seen from Sir James Ross's farthest in
1849, and retains, therefore, the name of Cape
Bird, given to it by that distinguished and accomplished officer.   On the south side of the entrance
of the channel is another conspicuous head-land,
to which I gave the name of Cape Hodgkin, in
honour of my esteemed friend Dr. Hodgkin of

London, who, I trust, will permit one of a race he has so largely benefited, to express this recognition of his unwearied exertions to elevate the condition of the native inhabitants of the Hudson's Bay territories.

In the course of the day we met with innumerable traces of rein-deer and musk-oxen, both old and recent, which led me to the conclusion that this is probably one of their principal "passes," in their annual migrations northward.

The country on each side of the passage is of primitive formation, bold and rocky, and rising towards the west and south into very high land.

Having satisfied ourselves that we were now upon the west side of North Somerset, it became a question how far the sea or channel before us might prove continuous with the opening laid down in our chart between Cape Walker and Cape Bunny. We had arrived at a point where, in pursuance of a plan I had the privilege of submitting to Lady Franklin before leaving England, the future direction of our route must be regulated by the appearance this western sea might present. If such as to afford a reasonable prospect of Franklin's having passed through to the south, our proper course would have been south also; but on examining the coast line to the northward, nothing could be seen but a continuous barrier of land extending from North Somerset to an extensive land which we could distinguish on the other side of the channel, and which we have since ascertained to be the Prince of Wales Land of Captain Ommanney. Having made it a rule to lay nothing down on our chart as land which had not been actually travelled over, the connexion between North Somerset and Prince of Wales Land does not appear in our map, in which the conspicuous headlands only have been inserted; but that a connexion does exist, or if it be broken by any passage or passages out of Peel Sound, that such passages are not navigable we had no doubt, and accordingly had no alternative but to proceed westward with the view of ascertaining whether any more promising channel existed farther west, through which Franklin might have penetrated from Cape Walker.

Thursday, 8*th.*—In pursuance of the decision come to yesterday, we struck due west across the channel, but owing to the rough ice, made very slow progress, and did not reach the opposite side till the 10th, after camping on the 8th and 9th on the floe. We had not been able, owing to the thickness of the weather, to make any extensive examination of the channel over which we had passed, but from the rough ice on each side appearing as if lodged by the tide, we inferred the existence of a current running north and south. Whether this current is derived from Prince Regent's Inlet through Bellot Strait, or from the Inlet between Cape Walker and Cape Bunny, through any passage or passages which may lead out of it, is a question of which we had no means of obtaining a satisfactory solution.

Saturday, 10*th.*—About noon we reached the west side of the channel, and found the land so low as scarcely to be distinguished from the floe we had been travelling over for the last two days. About an hour after striking the land we were arrested by a violent snow-storm that compelled us to camp at 2 P.M. in the middle of a wide plain. The difficulty of preserving a straight course, in an atmosphere through which earth, air, and sea appear all of a

colour, and in the total absence of any guiding land-
mark, can only be appreciated by those who have had
experience of such travelling as we had during this
and the two previous days. A compass, even if it
can be depended upon in latitudes so near the magnetic pole, cannot always be kept in the hand. In
our own case our course was guided almost entirely
by the wind, the direction of which was indicated by
a dog-vane carried in the hand.

The weather had been exceedingly cold for the last
few days, and to-day excessively so, and we were all
suffering severely from snow-blindness; the pain from
which, aggravated by the sharp particles of the snow-
drift dashed against our eyes by a furious head-wind,
was absolutely excruciating.

Sunday, 11*th*.—Continued in the encampment.
The storm raging without, with unabated violence.

Monday, 12*th*.—A lull in the storm induced us to
venture out about twelve o'clock. Our course was
still due west, in hourly expectation of falling upon
a western sea which might conduct us round to Cape
Walker. The country hitherto a dead flat, began to
shew an occasional elevation or rising ground, never,

however, entitled to the name of a hill; with the
exception of one solitary peak to which the name of
Mount Washington was given, in honour of Captain
Washington, R.N., a warm supporter of Arctic search,
a generous contributor to the outfit of the first Expedition of the Prince Albert, and the compiler of the
very useful Esquimaux vocabularies supplied to the
Arctic Expeditions.   We camped in the middle of a
plain, a few miles to the west of it.   To this plain
and the extensive level of which it formed part, and
over which we had been travelling for the last three
days, the name of Arrowsmith's Plains was given,
in honour of the eminent geographer to whom Arctic
discoverers are so much indebted.

Wednesday, 13th.—Still snowing, and the weather
very thick, which added to our snow-blindness, compelled us to camp at two P.M., after making a very
inconsiderable distance from our last encampment.

14th, 15th, 16th, and *17th.*—After several abortive
attempts to make head against the storm, found ourselves compelled to remain where we were.   Although
the loss of so much valuable time was a subject of
much regret to us all, the relief from exposure to

the glare of the snow was of great benefit to those affected with snow-blindness.

During this detention, and indeed on all other occasions of a similar nature throughout the journey, we restricted ourselves to one meal a day, and to save fuel ate our biscuit or pemmican with snow or ice instead of water, and by this means were enabled to make twenty-five days provision and fuel last thirty-five. The luxury of a cup of hot tea, and it was a luxury which we would not have exchanged for the wealth of Ophir, was reserved for our marching days. The flame of a gill and a half of spirits of wine was sufficient to boil a pint of tea for each of our party, and this quantity was duly measured out with the most scrupulous exactitude every morning and evening for breakfast and tea, excepting, of course, the banian days of our detention.

Sunday, 18*th.*—The weather clearing up, proceeded about eighteen miles still due west, through a somewhat hilly tract, intersected by ravines. The ground in detached spots was covered with heather and dwarf creeping willows. Numerous tracks of foxes were observed, all apparently proceeding northward.

A gaunt half-starved wolf followed us during the greater part of the day, but was eventually scared away by the repeated shots fired at him, none of which however, as far as we could see, took effect.

A meridian altitude, the first since coming on this new land, gave us the lat. 72° 1′ 48″ var. 155° 58′ 10.″

The thermometer at noon indicated + 22. A temperature which, to our sensations, was absolutely oppressive. One of our dogs through over-exertion, combined with the unusual heat, fainted in his traces, and lay gasping for breath for a quarter of an hour, but after recovering went on as merrily as ever. These faithful creatures were perfect treasures to us throughout the journey. They were all suffering like ourselves from snow-blindness, but did not in the least relax their exertions on this account. The Esquimaux dog is in fact the camel of these northern deserts—the faithful attendant of man, and the sharer of his labours and privations.

Monday, 19th.—A fine, but rather cloudy day. Started early, and towards the afternoon came upon a narrow but long lake, which extended N. and S. While the men were engaged in cutting the ice, I set off to its northern extremity to visit some objects, which at first appeared to be rein-deer or musk-oxen, but on being approached proved to be large stones on the top of some banks of gravel. On returning to the men I found they had dug the ice to a depth of four or five feet and found no water. A few musket balls were fired into the cavity, but no water was forthcoming, and the attempt was then abandoned. Having travelled to the usual camping hour, and all apparently feeling the benefit of our late four days' rest, we resolved from this time forward to travel during the night instead of the day, partly to avoid the fierce glare of the sun's rays and consequent snow-blindness, and partly, as we had felt the mid-day heat oppressive for steady marching, to secure the most bracing period of the twenty-four hours for walking. Accordingly, instead of erecting a snow-house, we threw up simply a snow-wall to windward, and seating ourselves round our conjuror, pannikin in hand, enjoyed a refreshing meal of pemmican and warm tea. This over we set out upon our night march, feeling as fresh as we did in the morning. The darkness of midnight we found a shade deeper than the day of mid-winter, but sufficiently light to permit our seeing our way quite clearly. With the advance of the morning of the 20th, we not only felt braced for duty, but were gratified with a sight of those lovely morning tints that herald the approach of day, and which forced the conviction on the mind rather that it was "morning when man goeth forth to his labour," than that we were drawing towards the close of a day's journey extended beyond the usual period.

Having marched till 9 A.M. of the 20th, we encamped, after performing a distance of not less than twenty-five miles due west, as nearly as we could estimate, for our compass had latterly been manifesting symptoms of sluggishness, which made it difficult at all times, with such heavy falls of snow as we had lately experienced, to keep a straight course.

Tuesday, 21st.—We had now, after another day's march of about twenty miles still due west, been thirteen days (including detentions) on this western land, and had reached a little beyond the 100th degree of W. longitude, without any indications of approaching the sea. Being now satisfied that Sir

James Ross had in his land journey along the western shore of North Somerset in 1849, mistaken the very low and level land over which we had been travelling for a western sea, I felt no longer justified in continuing a westerly course. Whatever passage might exist to the S. W. of Cape Walker, I felt assured must now be on our north. I determined, therefore, from this time forward to direct our course northward, until we should fall upon some channel which we knew must exist not far from us, in this direction, by which Franklin might have passed to the S.W. Accordingly, leaving our encampment of the 21st, about 10 P. M., we directed our steps due north, and after a march of twenty miles camped, on the forenoon of the 22nd, in the middle of a level plain, which had once more taken the place of the somewhat hilly district we had been travelling over for the last few days.

From the point where we turned northward, a conspicuous hill was seen to the west, to which the name of Mount Cowie was given, after the surgeon of the ship. A range of hills to the eastward received the name of Colquhoun Range, in honour of Col. Colquhoun of Woolwich, from whose instructions in the use of Copeland's blasting cylinders in the ice I had derived much benefit. To the solitary lake at the foot of the range which we had passed on the afternoon of the 19th, the name of Fisher's Lake was given, in honour of the Mayor of Hamilton, an active and influential friend of the Expedition in Canada.

Saturday, 24th.—Arrived at the bottom of a deep inlet, running apparently S. E. and N. W. which we have since ascertained to have been the Ommanney Bay of Capt. Austin's Expedition. The level plain over which we had been passing was observed here to give place to a range of high land, skirting the north shore of the Inlet as far as the eye could reach.

As yet we had not come upon the channel laid down upon our map as leading from Cape Walker, which lay at this time considerably to the north and east of our position. Our remaining resources would not admit of any extended explorations farther westward, and symptoms of scurvy were appearing amongst the men. I resolved, therefore, to turn eastward from this point, with the view of striking the channel, laid down to the east of Cape Bunny, and following it up to Cape Walker.

Tuesday, 27th.—After a difficult march of three days, in very thick weather, through a hilly tract of country from Ommanney Bay, we fell upon the low shelving shore of a deep bay in the channel we were in search of, and which appears in Capt. Austin's chart as Browne's Bay of Peel Sound. We found the tracks of rein-deer and musk-oxen here, much more numerous than had been observed on the western side of Prince of Wales Land,

John Smith and I made an endeavour to approach some deer which were quietly feeding upon the stunted heather, which, as already stated, forms almost the only vegetation of this barren district, in the manner adopted by the Indians of Hudson's Bay, by fixing our guns to the head, so as to give the appearance of horns, and crawling on all fours. We had succeeded in approaching within a fair distance for a shot, and were preparing to do execution upon them, when some movement of the sledges attracted their attention, and with a snuff of the air and a toss of their graceful antlers they bounded away, and were soon out of reach of our guns.

Speaking of native customs I may mention, that

having within the last few days killed some ptarmigan, and having no means of cooking them, we
followed the Indian practice of *freezing* them and
eating them raw. I can assure those who have not
tried the experiment that, though not equal to "perd-
rix rote," a frozen ptarmigan, after a hard day's
march, is by no means an unwelcome addition to an
Arctic traveller's bill of fare.

We had an incident of a different kind during the
forenoon of this same day. As I was proceeding in
advance of the party, with the view of selecting the
most level track for the sleighs, I was alarmed by a
cry from the men that Richard Webb's feet were
frozen. Sure enough, on placing the poor fellow on
the sleigh, and stripping off his mocassins, both feet
were as cold as two lumps of ice, and one already
slightly frozen. I immediately caused the men to
form a circle round him to protect him from the wind,
while John Smith and myself proceeded to restore
the circulation by rubbing the affected parts well over
with snow. This done I pulled out a pair of warm
dry mocassins, which I always carried under my belt
ready for next day's wear; and John Smith supplied

L

a pair of dry socks out of his bosom. As soon as these had been drawn on, and poor Dicky placed on his legs again, we were ready for a fresh start, and in less than a quarter of an hour we were all once more on our march, and our patient as lively and vigorous as ever. But to return from this digression.

The general appearance of the coast upon which we had fallen, readily accounted for Sir James Ross having laid it down in the Admiralty chart which had been supplied to us, as an extensive sea. The land was so uniformly low, and the headlands rose so abruptly from the general level in which they were situated, that seen from the coast of North Somerset, they could have assumed no other appearance to the most experienced eye than that of a sea studded with islands.

The general trending of this low coast appeared to be nearly due northward, and in the expectation of its leading to the long-sought for Cape Walker, we resolved thenceforth to follow it in that direction.

Tuesday, 4th.—By noon of this day the bold and conspicuous head-land of Cape Walker—the goal of our hopes and exertions for so long a period, was attained. Having ascertained since our return to England that the Inlet we had been coasting since the last date, had been previously explored with great care and minuteness by Lieut. Browne, under Capt. Ommanney's direction, I need not occupy the reader's attention with any description of this part of our route, which was unrelieved by any incidents of much interest in themselves. To Cape Walker we had confidently looked forward for some intelligence which would throw light upon the movements of Franklin's Expedition, had it passed in this direction to the S.W. as, from the tenor of the instructions under which it sailed from England, appeared not improbable. The remainder of this day and part of the next were accordingly devoted to a diligent examination of every spot within three miles on either side of the Cape, likely to have been selected for a cairn or staff, but without success; though Mr. Bellot carefully followed the windings of the rough ice outside the beach, in order to have a commanding view of the cliffs, whilst I searched along the sloping beach, and John Smith followed the base of the lofty cliffs, winding northward, which form Cape Walker.

The cairn, which I have learned since our return to England, was erected here by a party from the Expedition under Captain Austin, was not discovered by us owing to its resemblance in form to the numerous trap formations which are to be found throughout the country around the head-lands. I have also learnt from Captain Ommanney, that he himself erected a small cairn at the foot of Cape Walker, at which place he also buried a gutta-percha boat. I must conclude that these objects at the time we made our examination were covered with snow. My readers will draw from this fact, that the traces of a moving party may, and must often be overlooked, except at their winter-quarters or encampments.

Wearied and dispirited beyond description at the fruitless result of our long and anxious labours, we returned to our encampment, guided through a heavy snow-storm by the report of guns which I had directed to be fired every fifteen minutes, to make preparations for our return homeward. This could be effected either by pushing directly for Batty Bay, across North Somerset, a distance in a straight line of not more than six days' journey, or by following the coast round to Whaler Point, and thence to the ship. The latter route, though nearly double the actual distance of the other, appeared, on many grounds, to be preferable, and was accordingly that which we resolved on adopting.

Had it been possible for our small party to have carried a sufficient supply of provisions, for a more extended journey, we would most certainly have made a second excursion westward from Cape Walker. But we were now reduced to a supply that would barely suffice to carry us round the northern extremity of North Somerset to the depot at Whaler Point, which was still, at the lowest computation, eight or nine days march from us.

To lengthen out our stock of provisions, we fed our dogs on old leather shoes, and fag-ends of buffalo robes. To an Esquimaux dog nothing comes amiss, and on this fare they not only lived, but thrived wonderfully. An old snarling brute, that had been christened Boatswain by the men, and had been the plague of our voyage by his voracity and ill-temper, never enjoyed his grub, to judge from the fierce curl of his tail, till he was put upon this course of old shoes.

On the evening of the 5th we set out, in pursuance of the resolution at which we had arrived, to cross the opening between us and Cape Bunny, and, after travelling fifteen hours over very rough ice, camped midway, as was supposed, between Cape Walker and Limestone Island, which we reached on the forenoon of the 7th. The tracks of the deer and musk-oxen, so numerous on Prince of Wales' Land, had entirely disappeared as we approached the land of North Somerset, where, on the other hand, the traces of bears and foxes became very plentiful. On reaching the shore of North Somerset we followed the coast line, until we came nearly opposite Cunningham Inlet, when we struck straight for Cape Gifford, and on Sunday 9th camped near Cape Rennel. From this point we made a straight course for Cape Mc-Clintock, and encamped on the 10th near the west shore of Garnier Bay. On the following day we rounded Cape McClintock, where we unexpectedly came upon a small depot of provisions deposited here by Sir James Ross in 1849, as we learned on opening the cylinder left with the stores.

Within the last few days we had suffered so severely from scurvy, which had rendered us morbidly sensitive to cold and bodily fatigue, that although now only a day's journey from Whaler Point, we gladly availed ourselves of the opportunity which the accidental discovery of this depot afforded, to take a day or two's rest before proceeding farther.

We accordingly remained here until the afternoon of the 14th, when, though still suffering from the malady which had crippled some of us so greatly, we set out once more for Whaler Point, which we reached about 5 A.M. of the 15th.

On reaching this point we were gratified to find that Barrow's Strait was quite open in the direction of Lancaster Sound, and that the northern portion of Regent Inlet had also partially given way.

We remained at Whaler Point till the 27th, making a free use of the lime-juice, cranberries, vegetables, and, in fact, of every anti-scorbutic we found, so as to enable us the sooner to resume our

journey to the ship, where they must have been by
this time feeling anxious for our return.

The ice had so far opened from the shore as to give
us hopes of being able to reach Batty Bay by water,
but after proceeding as far as six or seven miles north
of Elwin Bay, in the gutta-percha boat, which had been
left here since last October, we were compelled to
abandon her, by the ice to the southward being still unbroken, and proceed for the remainder of the distance
on foot. By 5 A.M. of the 30th May, we reached the
ship, after an absence of ninety-seven days, during which
we had accomplished a journey of about 1100 miles.

Before leaving Whaler Point I deposited the
following notice of our proceedings for the information of any party that might touch there.

"This is to give notice that Lady Franklin's little
vessel, the 'Prince Albert,' has passed the winter of
1851-52 in Batty Bay, In January a party from
her visited Fury Beach and found no traces whatever
of Sir John Franklin or party. The stores landed
there however from the Fury still safe. In the
month of February, 1852, fourteen hands left the
Prince Albert again for Fury Beach. whence after some

preparations for a long journey southward, they took their final departure, on the 29th March. Their intention was, to have gone first to Brentford Bay, and then cross to the west, with a view to strike the supposed western sea of Sir James Ross, and then follow the coast down to the magnetic pole. After, however, travelling for about 100 miles into the interior, in a due west course, they found nothing but one uniform level plain, which it was supposed might lead to Banks' Land. As they had no means to enable them to reach this distant point, they turned northward (expecting to find a channel leading to the S.W.), up to Cape Walker, which they reached on the 4th of May; they found the land continuous, and gave it the name of Prince Albert Land. From Cape Walker, being short of provisions, they steered for this point, which they reached on the 15th of May. During the journey, not the smallest trace of Sir John Franklin was found. Cape Walker was carefully examined, but bore no evidence whatever of its having ever been visited by Europeans.

" Of the fourteen hands (including officers), which left Fury Beach, eight formed a fatigue party as far as Brentford Bay, from which they returned to the ship. The party, that performed the above journey, was composed of the following individuals : W. Kennedy, Lt. Bellot, John Smith, Andrew Irvine, Richard Webb, and W. Adamson, with five Esquimaux dogs.

"When they reached this point, they were all suffering so much from scurvy, that they had to delay here over a week in order to recruit. They are now (on the 25th May), ready to return to the ship, and only waiting for a change of the present boisterous weather. Regent's Inlet and Barrow's Strait, being quite open, as far as the eye can reach, they will proceed in the gutta-percha boat by water, as far as they can.

"After reaching the ship, the examination of the bottom of Grinnell Inlet (the Inlet west of North Somerset),* will form a first object—then probably

---

* It should be observed, that the naming of the Inlet west of North Somerset, was superseded by the *previous* discovery of this Inlet by Captain Ommanney, unknown of course to me, and so with many other names I had given to remarkable spots, all of which are now expunged from my chart.

Wellington Channel — that is, provided Sir John Franklin has not been traced in that direction.

" Any one finding this is respectfully requested to send a copy of this notice to Lady Franklin.

W. KENNEDY,

Commanding Lady Franklin's private Arctic Expedition."

CHAPTER VI.

HOMEWARD BOUND.

EXPLORATION OF CRESSWELL BAY, BY MR. COWIE——
PREPARATIONS FOR LEAVING WINTER HARBOUR——
SAWING OUT——LEAVE BATTY BAY——HEAVY DRIFT OF
ICE——FORCED INTO ELWIN BAY——GET A-GROUND——
PROCEED TOWARDS WELLINGTON CHANNEL——SIR
EDWARD BELCHER'S SQUADRON——PROPOSAL TO RE-
MAIN WITH THE NORTH STAR——BEAR AWAY FOR
ENGLAND——ARRIVAL AT ABERDEEN——RESULTS OF THE
EXPEDITION——POSITION AND PROSPECTS OF SIR JOHN
FRANKLIN AND THE MISSING SHIPS.

THERE was nothing in the occurrences at the ship
in the interval of our absence calculated to be of
much interest to the general reader, who is by this
time aware of the unavoidable monotony of a daily
routine life in winter quarters in the Arctic regions.
Suffice it to say that honest John Hepburn had
answered all my expectations while in charge of the
Prince Albert. The fatigue party sent back from
Brentford Bay had returned in safety, and had been
engaged from that time chiefly in ship duties, and I
regretted to find that many of them had suffered like

ourselves from scurvy, and were now still on the sick-
list. In pursuance of my instructions, Mr. Cowie
had examined Cresswell Bay, in order to ascertain
whether any communication existed between it and
the western sea ; but after a careful survey of the coast
line, both within and on each side of the bay, no
passage of the nature in question could be discovered.

Being now satisfied, from the long and laborious
explorations in which we had been engaged, that the
missing Expedition could not have been arrested
within any point attainable from Regent's Inlet, we
looked forward impatiently to the time when we
might be liberated from our present position, and be
enabled to enter upon a new field of search. As yet
there was little in the appearance of the ice or land
around us to indicate that the month of June had
arrived, beyond the falling in of some of the snow-
houses we had erected around the ship, and a
slight crusting of snow in situations exposed to the
sun. Gradually, however, the snow began to yield
before the fierce glare of the dog-days. Dark spots
of land shewed here and there on the hills, through
the general covering of white, and pools of water

began to form in the hollows of the ice, and to eat
their way through the holes and cracks.

By the beginning of July the snow had entirely
cleared off, and little rivulets pouring down constantly
from the hills were discharging their waters into the
bay, and lifting the ice bodily all around us. Seen
from the shore, the inlet presented the appearance
of a sea of dull-coloured glass, with long ridges like
the waves of an agitated ocean suddenly congealed,
and the whole rising and falling slowly with the tide.
An ingenious, though simple contrivance, enabled
us to measure the rise and fall of the tide throughout
the winter, for the ice had never been permanently
attached to the shore. A rope was lowered through
a fire-hole under the bowsprit, and anchored to the
bottom, while the other end was rove through a
pulley fixed above, with a weight attached, which, as
the ship rose and fell with the ice, indicated the
number of feet, by the descent of the weight. The
height of the tide, as thus indicated, ranged from
four to seven feet.

The most healthy of the men were in the meantime employed in bringing to the ship various

articles and remainders of deposits placed along the coast in the course of the winter and fall. Mr. Bellot made an excursion to Elwin Bay, to bring the little dingey left there on our journey from Port Leopold; but it had apparently somehow excited the wrath of a Polar bear, for, on arriving at it, the planking and timbers of one side were found completely torn away. This had been done apparently from pure wantonness, *pour passer le temps,* as no provisions, had been placed under it, or any where near it, either for man or beast.

The excursions for these objects over, some days were devoted to bringing on board a supply of water and ballast, and then followed a busy week or two of scrubbing and scouring, repairing and double stitching sails, trimming the rigging, caulking and pitching the deck, &c., until the little Albert looked once more as clean and bright as a new pin.

Last of all came a general washing on shore of all our clothing and bedding, which whitened the rocks far and near with rows of blankets, and all the heterogeneous items of an Arctic wardrobe,—and now behold us ready once more for sea, on the first peep of open water.

That most delightful of Arctic phenomena, more
precious to us than all the phenomena of all the 'ologies
in the " Penny Cyclopædia "—a water sky, had been
hanging over the Inlet for some time, and with the
view of ascertaining where the open water thus indicated lay, I proceeded with Mr. Bellot and eight hands
in the large mahogany boat, over the ice, with the determination of pushing on, if we could, as far as Port
Leopold, and bringing back the gutta-percha boat
left near Elwin Bay last May.   After a long drag, we
reached open water at 5 P.M. of the day on which
we left the ship (Thursday, 15th of July), and pulled
through it all night, reaching Port Leopold at noon
of the 16th.   On arriving here we had the gratification of finding Barrow's Strait and a part of Regent's
Inlet from Elwin Bay northward, quite free from ice.
We remained at our old familiar quarters at Whaler
Point for four days, busily occupied in removing some
of the stores, on which the sea appeared to be rapidly
encroaching, to a place of greater security. The beach
is crumbling away so rapidly that the launch, which
has its bow already projecting over high water-mark,
must, in a very short time, at this rate, be precipitated

into the sea and lost. The engine is much below the level of high water, and the anchor was already deeply imbedded in the sand some distance under the sea. The launch was so deeply imbedded in the frozen soil as to render it quite hopeless for our small party to attempt to move it, and such portions of the stores as we were able to remove, had to be dug out of a solid mass of ice and snow, which had formed about them.

On the morning of the 21st we set out on our return, and on the following day reached the ship with both the boats, which had again to be dragged over the ice from the north headland of Batty Bay, between which and Port Leopold we had been able to proceed by water very well.

The ice around the ship still continuing firm, the only prospect we had of liberating her, and getting into the open water, was by sawing a canal through the bay. Accordingly, the sawing apparatus was set going without delay, and although a very slow and laborious operation, cuts for a canal, half a mile in length, were completed in less than a week. Next came the process of clearing out; which, thanks to

M

the admirable invention of Copeland's blasting cylinders, was got through in gallant style. This invention, which promises to effect quite a revolution in the navigation of the icy seas, has only come into operation within the last few years, although it has, as I understand, long been practised on the Danube and other rivers of Germany, which are frozen over during the winter. One or more of these cylinders, according to the extent of the ice to be blasted, containing from 2 to 16lbs. of gunpowder, placed in a cut will shatter it in fragments, which the first ebb tide will float away, and when we reflect upon the old, harassing and tedious process of towing out the pieces of ice as they come from the saw, it will be a subject of surprise that this most useful invention has not long ago been put in practice by our Greenland whalers.

On the 6th of August, we were able to bid farewell to Batty Bay, which, after our long detention of 330 days, was anything but a subject of regret to us all. On getting through the canal, we found ourselves in a lane of comparatively open water, from five to six miles in breadth, extending between the pack and

the shore, (as far as we could observe from the crow's
nest,) nearly up to Cape Seppings. The wind was
unfortunately dead against us, and we had to tack
through this narrow channel for two days before we
could make the short distance to Elwin Bay, in which
we anchored in the evening of Sunday the 8th. Here
a sudden set of the ice into the bay drove us ashore,
and for two days we lay aground, exposed to immi-
nent danger from the constant stream of ice, which
at last entirely filled up the harbour. Although we
succeeded in getting the ship off without any evil
results from our mishap, we were detained here a
whole week, completely blocked in by a dense accumulation of ice across the mouth of the bay.

On Saturday the 14th, observing a narrow line of
open water between two extensive floes, we ventured
out of Elwin Bay, but had scarcely entered the lead
before we got entangled amongst the ice, and for the
next two days were driven about at the mercy of the
pack, without making an inch of advance northward,
but rather the reverse. On the 17th, by one of those
sudden and inexplicable movements, so common in
the navigation of these seas, the ice had in a great

measure cleared away, and we found ourselves beating up against a strong head wind, through comparatively open water, for Beechey Island, which we reached on the morning of the 19th. Shortly after 6 A.M., being then a little to the S. E. of Cape Riley, a ship was reported in sight, which proved to be H.M. Ship North Star, from England, sawing into winter-quarters.

From Commander Pullen we learned, with infinite gratification, that a squadron of five vessels, of which the North Star formed one, under Sir Edward Belcher's orders, had been despatched by the Admiralty, during the present season, to follow up the important discoveries of traces of Sir John Franklin's Expedition at Beechey Island. The two divisions of the squadron, under Sir Edward Belcher, C.B. and Captain Kellett, C.B. had passed on through clear water a few days before,—the one—consisting of Sir Edward Belcher's own ship the "Assistance," with the "Pioneer," steam tender, Commander Sherard Osborn,—to explore the promising Queen's Channel discovered by Penny, beyond the Wellington Channel,—and the other—the "Resolute," Captain Kellett's ship, with the "Intrepid," steam tender, Commander M'Clintock, to proceed towards Melville Island.

Dr. M'Cormick, that most enterprising of Arctic voyagers—who was with Parry in the north, and with Sir James Ross in the south—had gone up the Wellington Channel in a boat, to Baring Bay, intending thence, if possible, to cross the land to the eastward, and strike upon Jones' Sound to the spot where the 'Prince of Wales' had reported a cairn to have been seen, with foot-prints, &c. His return was shortly expected.

By the North Star I had a letter from Lady Franklin, left for me by Sir Edward Belcher, in which she requested me to place myself and her little vessel under Sir Edward Belcher's orders, if he desired it, and the health of the crew and the quantity of my remaining provisions permitted me to do so. This was of course now impossible, and in his absence I made the offer of the Prince Albert to Commander Pullen, who felt himself, however, precluded by the general orders to the squadron from availing himself of it.

Relying, however, upon the general instructions of the Admiralty, that we were to receive every necessary assistance from Sir Edward Belcher which we might stand in need of, Captain Pullen very kindly placed at my disposal an officer and three men, as soon as he found that Mr. Bellot and myself were anxious to remain out another season, in order to complete the remaining part of the search, which I had originally planned for myself. The greater part of my own men were not sufficiently recovered from the effects of their former labours and privations to be fit for renewed exertion, till after a farther period of rest and restorative treatment. I determined, therefore, to send the Prince Albert back to England, under charge of Mr. Leask; since to spend the whole of that remaining season and next winter idle would be a wasteful expenditure of provisions, for which there was no equivalent advantage. Two of the men, John Smith and Kenneth Sutherland, volunteered to remain behind, and start afresh with me and Bellot, on our projected exploration; and with this view a supply of food and fuel, and other needful things commensurate with our expected

wants, was put on board the North Star, sufficient
to last us another year. We had at this time
abundant provisions to last the whole ship's company for a twelvemonth. But our plans were not
destined to be realized. On being made acquainted
with the nature of the Admiralty regulations, to
which they would be subjected by their removal
to the North Star, first Sutherland, and subsequently Smith, withdrew their offer, alleging, as a
farther reason for their change of purpose, their
fears, which I found were shared by the Prince
Albert's crew in general, that the fresh men from
England would not be able to bear the same fatigue
as themselves, some of whom had been all their lives
more or less at this hard exploring labour. Mr.
Bellot and myself were thus most reluctantly compelled to abandon our enterprise, and the disappointment seemed to be scarcely less felt by that fine
young officer, Mr. Alston, of H.M.S. North Star,
who had so nobly desired to be the companion of our
future adventures.

The provisions we had placed on board the North
Star were again shifted to Beechey Island, to be

stored in the house there being constructed, and to
be at the disposal of the squadron. We left behind
the gutta-percha boat, which had been so invaluable
to us, the small boat, or dingey, some tons of fuel,
pemmican, biscuit, preserved provisions, and other
stores in considerable quantities, sufficient for the
rations of four men for a year and more, our Esquimaux dogs, and lastly, the organ, which had been
so graciously presented by H. R. H. Prince Albert,
and which had so often cheered us during our icy
imprisonment. Feeling that the loneliness of the
North Star as a depôt, and therefore comparatively
inactive ship, gave her claims upon our sympathy, I
left this precious gift, on condition that it should be
carefully returned.

We had brought out in the Prince Albert from
three to four hundred letters, addressed for the most
part to the officers and men of Captain Austin's
squadron, which in the mean time had returned
home. A portion of these, for such of the crews
of the late squadron as had returned with Sir
Edward Belcher, being deposited with Commander
Pullen, we bore away for Britain on the 24th of

CAPE RILEY

HOMEWARD BOUND FROM BEECHY ISLAND

J. COVENTRY, LITH.

August, under three hearty cheers from the North
Star, carrying with us the latest despatches to the
Admiralty from Sir Edward Belcher's squadron, and
the most cheering intelligence of their prospects of
success.

We left Commander Pullen still busy with the
work of securing himself in winter harbour, and in
the construction of a wooden house on Beechey
Island for the reception of stores.   This Arctic
dwelling was to be called Northumberland House,
and if of less noble proportions than the mansion
of his Grace the late First Lord of the Admiralty at
Charing Cross, it will be unapproachable in size and
magnificence in those regions, standing "alone in
its glory;" and instead of one proud lion erect on
its summit, there are inexhaustible quarries of
Arctic alabaster all around, from which they may
carve as many as they please to encircle and guard it.

From Beechey Island we steered for Navy Board
Inlet, with the hope of being able, on our arrival in
England, to report to the Admiralty the state of the
stores there.   After two unsuccessful attempts, however, to reach it, we were compelled to abandon our

intention and resume our course homeward. Commander Sherard Osborn had previously attempted, but was unable to discover the spot where Mr. Saunders had landed the provisions from the North Star.

And here I may be permitted to remark upon the futility, as I fear it will prove, of placing depôts of provisions upon the south, instead of upon the north shore of Barrow Strait ; an opinion entertained and clearly stated by Sir Edward Belcher.

A succession of favouring gales bore us rapidly across the Atlantic, notwithstanding some vexatious obstructions from the middle ice in Baffin's Bay. By the 21st of September we were off Cape Farewell, and in twelve days more had sighted St. Kilda. Thence we bore away round the north coast of Scotland by the Pentland Frith, and on the afternoon of Thursday, the 7th of October, anchored in Aberdeen harbour, exactly six weeks from the commencement of our homeward-bound voyage, and after an absence altogether of sixteen months from England.

I cannot close this brief narrative of a voyage, accomplished under unusual difficulties, and in the

absence of many appliances possessed by others
engaged in the prosecution of an extensive exploration of the Arctic Seas, without according here,
first my gratitude to the Almighty for the protection
He has in His mercy vouchsafed to us; and my
obligations to the officers and crew of our little vessel,
by whose hardihood, preseverance, and uniform good
conduct alone we were enabled to effect what we
did. To Mr. Bellot, my constant companion, not
only do I owe the most valuable assistance from his
scientific attainments, but his amiable qualities have
cemented a deep personal regard which can end only
with my life. Out of 330 days, during which we
were detained in winter-quarters, many of the
men were out nearly one half the time, and this in
the depth of mid-winter, journeying through incessant
snow-storms, and a temperature such as I believe no
marching party has ever before been called upon to
encounter in the Arctic regions. During this time
some of them must have travelled fully 2000 miles.
After such severe and protracted exertion, it was with
inexpressible satisfaction that I had the happiness of
seeing every one of these brave fellows return to

their native country, in as robust health as when they left it sixteen months before, with the exception of three unimportant cases on our sick list.

Although, as the reader is aware, some of the explorations were carried on over parts previously visited (though unknown to us) by others of Captain Austin's squadron, I am glad to believe, for the sake of those by whose arduous labours they were accomplished, that the results of our Expedition will not, even in a geographical view, be without some interest, as a contribution to the charts of the Polar Seas and Regions, our whole knowledge of which has been gained during the last three centuries, step by step, by indomitable perseverance, singleness of purpose, and the most noble spirit of enterprise—to which, in our present Arctic researches we may add, the sacred call of humanity. Our chief acquisition in geography may be stated in a few words — the discovery of a passage from Regent's Inlet to the Victoria Channel of Rae, thereby supplying an important link in establishing the existence of a north-west passage along the northern shores of America, actually accomplished by the united labours

of British navigators. To this may be added the determination of the physical aspect of the extensive
land lying to the west of North Somerset, and the
contribution of some additional facts regarding its
various coast lines. Geography, however, as I need
hardly say, was not our object. Important, as under
other circumstances such would doubtless have been,
ours was indeed a far nobler one,—to rescue, or solve
the fate of our long-absent countrymen. Although unsuccessful in its attainment, the result of our explorations, as shewing at least where the missing expedition
is *not*, will, I trust, not have been without its use as a
contribution to the solution of this important and
deeply-interesting question. Added to the Explorations of those who have preceded us in the same
direction in the field of search, I think there can be
but little doubt that Franklin has *not* gone by Cape
Walker, but has taken the northern route, through
the Queen's Channel and Penny Strait, and proceeded to an advanced west longitude, and is now to
be sought for from the westward, or Behring Strait.
Of the interest and importance of the immense field
of search opened to us by recent discoveries, and
into which Franklin has no doubt proceeded far to

the westward, we are only now becoming aware. It seems, indeed, that the very conditions under which an opinion favourable to the safety of the missing Expedition can be sustained, are its having advanced to a remote position in some high latitude, and its detention there, either by wreck or imprisonment in the ice, and continued up to this time, by the absence of means to overcome the distance to be traversed, before inhabited, or frequented regions, can be reached.

As regards the means of sustaining life in these regions, perhaps no fact has been better established by the observations and experience of the various Expeditions which have left England within the last few years;—while the worst founded apprehensions in relation to our missing countrymen is that based upon the imagined want of food. On this subject I cannot forbear quoting the following excellent remarks (with which I entirely concur), from a lecture delivered at Washington by my valued and accomplished friend Lieut. Kane, of the United States' searching Expedition, fitted out by that prince of merchants, Mr. Grinnell of New York.

" Nor is there any reason to apprehend that the

missing party has perished from cold, or starvation, or disease. The Igloe or snow-house of the Esqui-maux is an excellent and wholesome shelter. The servants of the Hudson's Bay Company preferred it to the winter hut; and for clothing the furs of the Polar regions are better than any of the products of Manchester. The resources which that region evi-dently possesses for the support of human life, are certainly surprisingly greater than the public are generally aware of. Narwhal, white whale and seal, the latter in extreme abundance, crowd the waters of Wellington Channel, indeed it was described as a ' region teeming with animal life.' The migrations of the eider-duck, the brent goose, and the auk—a bird about the size of our teal—were absolutely won-derful. The fatty envelope of these marine animals, known as blubber, supplies light and heat, their furs warm and well adapted clothing, their flesh whole-some and anti-scorbutic food. The rein-deer, the bear, and the fox, also abounded in great numbers even in the highest latitudes attained; add to all this, that the three years provisions which Franklin carried out, was calculated according to the pro-verbial liberality of the British Admiralty, and was

indeed abundant for a support during four years and
a half, and that he was the man of all others whom
necessity had taught the lesson of husbanding his
resources, and of adding to them when occasion permitted ; and we have a summary of what might be
made a conclusive reply to the apprehensions on the
score of a want of food."*

With such an array of encouraging facts and reasoning, we have everything to stimulate us to a continuance of those efforts for the relief of Franklin
and his devoted followers, to which the wonderful
proofs continually acquired of the existence of animal
life, in regions so long supposed to be destitute of it,
are imparting a character of ever-increasing hope.

Nor is it the least gratifying circumstance to the
friends of Arctic search that such views are finding a
wide and general acceptance among the most eminent
of our men of science.   In a speech of the Rev. Dr.
Robinson, Dean of Armagh, (while reviewing the
business of the different sections) at the late meeting
of the British Association for the Advancement of

* Quoted from the "Papers and Despatches relating to the Arctic
Searching Expeditions," collected and arranged by Captain Mangles
one of the most valuable publications which has appeared on the subject of Franklin's Expedition.

Science, at Belfast, I find the following observations, in reference to a paper on the Zoology of the Polar Regions by Mr. Petermann :—

" From the abundance of animal life in those regions, there is no reason to doubt the safety of men so energetic, so fearless, and so true to their officers and themselves, as that noble band of our country-men, about whose welfare or whose existence every right-minded man is anxious, who accompanied Franklin on his last expedition, unless they have been the victims of some casualty by which both the ships of the expedition were instantly destroyed; for they were certain to find an ample and abundant means of sustaining life with both fuel and food. It was an exceedingly interesting paper, and not rendered less so by the discussion which it produced. One of our naturalists was rather disposed to doubt the high probability to which I allude, and I was glad when the discussion called up Owen and Murchison, and our President, Colonel Sabine—one who had passed through all the perils of the Arctic voyage, and is perfectly aware, by his own experience, of all the dangers of an Arctic winter. Perhaps I can add

N

nothing to what Colonel Sabine said, when asked, did he think our countrymen could exist in the rigour of those Polar regions? 'The Esquimaux,' said he, 'live there; and, where they live, Englishmen can live!' That contained the whole solution of the question. These men would have energy, some resources, and, above all, nothing could deprive them of the unconquerable courage and warmhearted devotion to each other which ever was, and ever will be, the character of British sailors. And, when these gentlemen expressed their assurance and conviction, that it was the bounden duty of the Government never to rest till they obtained certain information of the death of Franklin and his followers, or certain evidence of their existence—when they said that public opinion would never cease to impress and force the necessity of this their bounden duty on the Government—I felt, from the cheer that echoed the sentiment, that it was impossible but that the expectation would be realised to the fullest extent."

APPENDIX.

CORRESPONDENCE WITH THE ADMIRALTY, AND WITH THE FRENCH BOARD OF MARINE AND COLONIES, RELATIVE TO THE EXPEDITION IN THE "PRINCE ALBERT."

Letter from Mr. W. Kennedy to the Secretary of the Admiralty.

Admiralty, in waiting, 9th October, 1852.

SIR,

I BEG to inform you of my arrival with the "Prince Albert" from the Arctic seas, having reached Aberdeen on Thursday evening at 6 P. M.

I left the "North Star," Captain Pullen, at Beechey Island, taking up her winter quarters, all well on board.

Dr. M'Cormick had just launched his boat in open water, with a party I think of four men, and was proceeding to Baring Bay, to ascertain if there was any opening to the eastward into Jones's Sound, with a view of examining the cairn and cooking-place seen by the "Prince of Wales" in 1848.

I arrived at Beechey Island on the 19th of August, and quitted on the 24th.

Sir Edward Belcher, with one tender, the " Pioneer," Lieutenant (now Commander) Sherard Osborn, had proceeded up the Wellington Channel in open water a few days previous to my arrival, while Captain Kellett with the other tender, Captain M'Clintock, had gone in clear water up Barrow Straits towards Melville Island.

The " Prince Albert " wintered in Batty Bay, Prince Regent Inlet.

In January, accompanied by M. Bellot of the French Navy, I proceeded with a sledge and three men, alike to visit Fury Beach and to form a first depôt.

Returning to the ship, we again started in February, myself in charge of an advance party of five men, and M. Bellot the week following in charge of a party of seven men, having left Messrs. Hepburn and Leask in charge of the ship.

On M. Bellot coming up with me at Fury Beach, I found it necessary to send him back again to the ship, in order to bring down further supplies, and it was not until the 29th of March that we were enabled to proceed on the extended journey. A fatigue party accompanied us as far as Brentford Bay ; here we found an opening running in a general course of about S. W. and N. E. of about fifteen miles to Cape Bird; on attaining Cape Bird crossed a bay of some twenty-five miles in width, when we struck a low-lying beach, and pursued our course on it over gentle undulations, in a direction due west, of the estimated distance of 100º W. longitude. On the third day we got on flat table-land until the latitude of 73º N. when we turned east, and struck the Inlet west of N. Somerset.

Our course was now generally along the sea-coast until we reached Cape Walker, when our provisions compelled us to retreat to the ship round N. Somerset and Leopold Harbour.

I cannot find words to express my admiration of the conduct of M. Bellot, who accompanied me throughout this trying journey, directing at all times the course by his superior scientific attainments, and at the same time taking an equal share with the men in dragging the sled, and ever encouraging them in their arduous labours by his native cheerful disposition.

During our absence of three months, we ever slept in snow houses, having dispensed with tents.

With the blessing of God, we returned in safety to our ship on the 30th of May.

On the 6th of August we cut out of winter quarters

and proceeded to Beechey Island, as circumstances best directed.

I may mention, that our first journey was in mid-winter, when we had to avail ourselves of the moonlight, in the absence of that of the sun.

I have, in conclusion, the satisfaction to remark, that although our crew suffered somewhat from scurvy, they have all returned to a man in comparative health, which I attribute in a great measure to the strictly teetotal principles on which the expedition was carried out, and the consequent harmony and good conduct of the men throughout.

It is to the supply of pemmican, which the Lords of the Admiralty liberally supplied to the "Prince Albert," that our sled journies were enabled to be carried out; I left 18 cases of pemmican at Beechey Island, and two at Fury Beach, and four tons of coal I put on board the "North Star."

During my absence on the extended journey, Mr. Cowie, the medical officer, searched the bottom of Cresswell Bay, to see if any passage existed there, but found none; to this officer I also feel greatly indebted for his care and attention over the health of the crew, and kind and skilful treatment of them.

Though every search was made in all parts we have visited, we have found no record or trace of the proceedings of Sir John Franklin's expedition.

I have, &c.

(signed)   WM. KENNEDY,

Commanding Lady Franklin's Private
Arctic Expedition.

———————

Letter from the Secretary of the Admiralty to Mr. W. Kennedy.

Admiralty, 15 October, 1852.

SIR,

I HAVE received and laid before my Lords Commissioners of the Admiralty your letter of the 9th inst., reporting your arrival from the Arctic Seas, and I am to acquaint you that my Lords are greatly obliged for the valuable information you have been the means of conveying to them from the squadron under Captain Sir E. Belcher's orders, and their Lordships have further to thank you for the interesting detail of your own proceedings. My Lords would wish to express their sense of the exertion made by you, and your arduous efforts to discover traces of the missing expedition, and would be glad, should the opportunity offer, if you would convey to your gallant comrade, M. Bellot, the like assurance of their Lordships' admiration of the generous ardour with which that officer's valuable services were devoted to the humane and honourable enterprise in which you were both engaged.

I am, &c.

(signed)   W. A. B. HAMILTON.

Letter from the Secretary of the Admiralty to H. U. Addington, Esq., Foreign Office.

Admiralty, 15 October, 1852.

SIR,

I AM commanded by my Lords Commissioners of the Admiralty to send you herewith, for the information of the Earl of Malmesbury, copies of a letter from Mr. W. Kennedy, dated 9th instant, reporting his arrival from the Arctic Seas, and of one which I have this day by their Lordships' commands addressed to him ; and I am to request you will inform Lord Malmesbury that my Lords have transmitted the same, in order (if his Lordship should see fit) that the French Government may be made acquainted with M. Bellot's generous exertions in

behalf of British officers and men, and the opinion entertained of him by their Lordships.

I am directed to add that M. Bellot is Lieutenant de
Vaisseau in the French navy, and Chevalier of the Legion
of Honour.

I have, &c.

(signed)   W. A. B. HAMILTON.

---

*Letter from Mr. W. Kennedy to the Secretary of the
Admiralty.*

East Islington Institution,
18 October, 1852.

SIR,

I HAVE had the honour to receive your letter of
the 15th instant, conveying to Lieutenant Bellot of the
French navy and myself the thanks of the Board of
Admiralty, for the information which we have had the
happiness to communicate in respect to the proceedings
of Sir Edward Belcher's squadron, and the expression
of their Lordships' approbation of our humble exertions
to afford assistance to our long absent countrymen in
the expedition under the command of Sir John Franklin.

May I request that you will assure their Lordships, on the part of Lieutenant Bellot and myself, that we feel deeply gratified at so honourable a mark of their Lordships' approbation, which is in itself a high reward to us for the arduous service upon which we have been engaged.

I have, &c.

(Signed)   WM. KENNEDY,

Late commanding Lady Franklin's
Private Arctic Expedition.

Lady Franklin to the Secretary of the Admiralty.

LADY FRANKLIN presents her compliments to the Secretary of the Admiralty, and begs to enclose the copy of a letter which she has had the gratification of receiving from his Excellency the Minister of Marine of France, in compliment to Lieutenant Bellot of the French Navy.

37, *Bedford Place,*
1 *November*, 1852.

(Translation.)

Paris, 25 October, 1852.

MADAM,

I HAVE received the letter which you did me the honour to address to me on the 20th instant.

The French Government could do no less than give its cordial assent to the desire expressed by M. Bellot, Lieutenant de Vaisseau, to join the expedition in search of the noble and unfortunate Sir John Franklin, which proceeded in the ship " Prince Albert."

In rendering himself worthy of receiving from you, Madam, whose devotion is the admiration of the whole world, the expressions of esteem conveyed in your letter, and in earning by the energy and usefulness of his participation in an enterprise as perilous as honourable, the suffrages of the British Admiralty, M. Bellot has gained fresh claims to the consideration of his superiors, whose trust he has so fully justified, and to the esteem of the corps to which he belongs, and which he has so worthily represented.

In the name of the French Navy, I sincerely invoke success for the new expedition which has succeeded the

" Prince Albert," and that it may attain the object
which you follow with so much courageous perseverance.

Accept, Madam, the homage of my profound respect.

The Minister of Marine and Colonies,

(Signed)   THEODORE DUCOS.

Lady Franklin, London.

METEOROLOGICAL JOURNAL ON BOARD THE PRINCE ALBERT FOR JULY, 1851.

Date.	Thermom.				Wind.	Lat.	Long.	Remarks.
	8 a.m.	Noon.	4 a.m.	8 a.m.				
Tues. 1	.	..	..	..	s. & s.w.			
Wed. 2								
Thurs. 3								
Frid. 4	.	..	..	..	E.N.E.	off Hare	Island.	foggy and clear.
Sat. 5	30	33	31	30	E.N.E.	....	....	dense fog workg. nrthd.
Sund. 6	..	40	36	34	N.w.&var.	....	....	greater part foggy.
Mon. 7	..	38	..	34	N.N.W.	71° 09'	....	cloudy and clear.
Tues. 8	..	39	..	..	N.N.W.	....	....	clear weather.
Wed. 9	..	44	..	.	N.N.E.	off Law	son ld.	clear and cloudy.
Thur. 10	..	41	..	..	s.s.F.	Apperna	vich.	clear and fine.
Frid. 11	..	55	..	46	variable.	....	....	serene pleasant weather.
Sat. 12	..	42	..	..	s.s.w. & F.	off Sugar-	loaf.	generally clear.
Sund. 13	..	38	..	..	s.s.w.	near Baf	fin's lds.	hazy and rain.
Mon. 14	..	43	..	..	calm.	at same	place.	foggy.
Tu.s. 15	.	45	..	..	calm.	....	....	generally overcast.
Wed. 16	..	41	..	.	light var.	Baffin's	Islands.	fine serene weather.
Thur. 17	..	44	..	..	s.w. fresh.	Baffin's	Islands.	clear.
Frid. 18	..	60	57	48	light var.	N. of Baf	fin's lds.	generally clear and mild.
Sat. 19	..	49	37	33	s.w strong	off Wilcox	Point.	cloudy.
Sund. 20	37	41	39	37	calm.	in sight of	Dev. thb.	cloudy and clear.
Mon. 21	37	38	37	34	N.E light.	off Devil's	thumb.	cloudy and rain.
Tues. 22	40	46	41	..	variable.	....	....	clear.
Wed. 23	43	46	46	42	N.E & calm	....	....	overcast.
Thur. 24	48	55	49	43	calm.	....	....	clear.
Frid. 25	39	48	42	37	calm & var	....	....	clear.
Sat. 26	37	40	39	28	s.F. light.	....	....	foggy and overcast.
Sund. 27	37	40	38	34	variable.	....	....	rain and cloudy.
Mon 28*	33	33	33	33	s.s.E.gale.	....	....	{ heavy rain and cloudy { sun eclip. but not seen.
Tues. 29	36	45	38	37	s.F. fresh.	....	....	generally clear.
Wed. 30	39	43	..	35	s.E.&s.s.E	....	....	clear throughout.
Thur. 31	36	39	33	31	southerly.	....	....	occasion. snow showers.

* Mond. 28th, having a total eclipse of the sun, thermom. stood at 33o all day, and had much heavy rain.

METEOROLOGICAL JOURNAL FOR AUGUST, 1851.

Date.	8 a.m.	Noon	4 p.m.	8 a.m.	Wind.	Lat.	Long.	Remarks.
Frid. 1	36	40	..	32	southerly.	off Devil's	Thumb.	clear fog & snow shws.
Sat. 2	29	36	32	31	northerly.	......	....	clr.clm.& light n.wind
Sund. 3	38	43	37	32	ditto.	....	....	variable and clear.
Mon. 4	39	45	42	33	ditto.	....	....	foggy.
Tues. 5	38	43	38	35	n.&e.s.e.	....	....	cloudy.
Wed. 6	37	41	40	36	s.s.e&n.n.w	....	....	cloudy.
Thurs. 7	37	41	47	36	variable.	....	....	rain and snow.
Frid. 8	37	41	42	41	n.n.e.	....	....	clear.
Sat. 9	37	40	41	34	e. & s.e.	....	....	rain and fog.
Sund. 10	39	43	41	36	n.e.n.&n.w.	....	....	hazy and clear.
Mon. 11	37	46	38	43	n.w.	....	....	clear.
Tues. 12	41	43	51	44	n.e.	....	....	clear.
Wed. 13	39	43	39	31	variable.	....	....	foggy.
Thur. 14	29	30	30	29	s.	....	....	dense fog.
Frid. 15	29	30	32	30	s.s.w.	....	....	frequent snw. showers
Sat. 16	35	40	40	38	southerly.	......	....	fog and rain.
Sund. 17	35	41	47	41	n.e.	off Baf	fin's 3 Ids.	clear.
Mon 18	28	29	30	29	variable.	72o 30'	....	clear and foggy.
Tues. 19	31	31	23	30	variable.	gng. thro'	mid. ice.	haze and snow shwrs.
Wed. 20	27	28	29	29	s.s.w.	gng. thro'	mid. ice.	fog and snow showers.
Thur.21	30	38	35	31	s.e & e.	} got thr. mid.ice / { 73o 15'	64o 57'	haze&light snw.shws.
Frid. 22	29	36	38	32	n. & n.w.	73o 15'	64o 4'	clear weather.
Sat. 23	30	34	36	30	variable.	73o 10'	64o 00"	clear and foggy.
Sund.24	28	33	34	30	northerly.	......	....	thick fog and clear.
Mon. 25	26	30	32	28	calm.	off C.Gra.	Moore.	generally cloudy.
Tues. 26	38	38	38	36	calm.	off Cape	Burney.	generally clear.
Wed. 27	36	37	35	36	calm & var.	off Poss	ession Bay	fog and heavy rain.
Thur.28	35	36	38	36	variable.	off By. M	arten In.	clear.
Frid. 29	34	33	35	26	n.n.e.	off Navy	Bd. In.	rain and fog.
Sat. 30	33	34	35	32	w.n.w.&n.w	......	....	...... &strong gale.
Sund.31	31	31	35	33	westerly.	.. C.Wa	render.	hazy snow and sleet.

METEOROLOGICAL JOURNAL FOR SEPTEMBER, 1851.

Date.	8 a.m.	Noon.	4 p.m.	8 p.m.	Wind.	Lat.	Long.	Remarks.
Mon. 1	30	32	33	29	E. by s.	off Admi	ralty Inl.	cloudy and strong gale
Tues. 2	31	33	34	30	easterly.	....	....	....
Wed. 3	28	30	33	29	....	enter Re	gent Inlet	fog and haze. [shws.
Thurs. 4	29	31	35	30	N.E.	off Point	Leopold.	cloudy, clear, & snow
Frid. 5	28	30	33	29	N.E.	enter Pt.	Bowen.	generally clear.
Sat. 6	29	30	31	30	calm.	at Point	Bowen.	....
Sund. 7	3(	32	36	30	N.N.W.	....	.. ....	clear and cloudy.
Mon. 8	30	31	33	28	w. and var.	cross for	Pt. Leop.	clear and cloudy.
Tues. 9	28	30	31	29	N.W. strong.	off Cape	Seppings.	frequent snow shwrs.
Wed. 10	28	29	30	26	w.w. strong.	{ ent.Barry Bay. { to winter.		cloudy and snow shws.
Thur. 11	22	29	27	25	northerly.	....	....	clear.
Frid. 12	26	29	30	31	variable.	....	....	clear.
Sat. 13	32	37	26	23	westerly.	....	....	clear, mild weather.
Sund. 14	19	25	29	29	s.s.E.	....	....	dark, cloudy weather.
Mon. 15	33	34	32	25	w.n.w.	....	....	rain and snow shwrs.
Tues. 16	22	26	24	22	N.w. by w.	strong	gale.	heavy snow drift.
Wed. 17	20	22	22	17	....	....	.. ....	....
Thur. 18	21	24	24	20	....	....	... .	....
Frid. 19	21	25	24	22	w.N.w.	strong	....	clear.
Sat. 20	21	27	29	26	variable.	....	....	cloudy and snow drift.
Sund. 21	19	18	17	19	w.N.w.	strong gale.		clear.
Mon. 22	18	17	4	13	w.N.w.	strong gale.		cloudy and snow drift.
Tues. 23	11	32	23	19	light N.	......	.....	clear.
Wed. 24	19	20	19	18	s.E. light.	....	....	clear.
Thur. 25	23	26	26	21	s.F. and N.	....	....	heavy snow.
Frid. 26	15	18	15	18	variable.	....	....	fine and clear.
Sat. 27	16	24	17	12	N	mod. and strong.		clear and snow drift.
Sund. 28	12	14	13	10	N.	moderate.		fine and clear.
Mon. 29	8	11	8	5	N.	light.	....	light snow showers.
Tues. 30	11	12	11	10	N.	moderate.	......	hazy & snow showers.

METEOROLOGICAL JOURNAL FOR OCTOBER, 1852.

Date.	Thermom.				Wind.	Remarks.
	8 a.m.	Noon.	4 p.m.	8 p.m.		
Wed. 1	13	12	10	7	northerly.	Gloomy and downcast.
Thurs. 2	10	11	10	6	ditto.	Fine and clear.
Frid. 3	9	11	1:	5	ditto.	Clear.
Sat. 4	7	8	9	7	southerly.	Cloudy.
Sun. 5	0	9	5	3	north.	Fine and clear.
Mon. 6	5	7	6	6	ditto.	Generally clear.
Tues. 7	13	15	10	8	ditto.	Clear throughout.
Wed. 8	13	15	13	10	ditto.	Clear and cloudy.
Thur. 9	13	20	25	15	n.and calm.	Fine and clear.
Frid. 10	12	18	23	9	variable.	Clear and cloudy.
Sat. 11	7	9	7	3	w.n.w.&w.	Clear.
Sund.12	10	12	8	3	n. & w.	Clear.
Mon. 13	6	10	3	0	n.	Clear.
Tues. 14	3	6	4	2	n.-westerly	Clear.
Wed. 15	—3	0	—1	—3	n.w.	Fine clear weather.
Thur.16	0	3	5	8	n.w.	Dull and cloudy.
Frid. 17	15	16	18	16	variable.	Cloudy and snow showers.
Sat. 18	12	14	16	8	ditto.	Snow and drift.
Sund.19	16	12	12	13	s.e.	Cloudy and snow drift.
Mon. 20	7	5	4	1	e.s.e.	Cloudy and overcast. [drift.
Tues.21	2	5	4	4	s.e.	Clear and cloudy with snow
Wed. 22	7	9	11	17	s.e. strong.	Cloudy, snowing, and drift.
Thur.23	20	24	26	27	s.s.e.	Snowing all day.
Frid. 24	26	24	24	24	s.s.e.	Thick haze and snow drift.
Sat. 25	25	25	25	23	variable.	Clear and overcast.
Sund.26	21	21	23	15	s.s.e.	Dull, hazy weather.
Mon. 27	8	13	14	17	easterly.	Cloudy.
Tues. 28	15	18	15	10	ditto.	Cloudy and snow drift.
Wed. 29	-3	—8	—5	—1	e.s.e.&n.n.e	Cloudy and snow drift.
Thur.30	—2	—4	—7	—8	e n.e.	Snow and drift.
Frid. 31	—10	—10	—5	-- 6	easterly.	Clear throughout.

METEOROLOGICAL JOURNAL FOR
NOVEMBER, 1851.

Date.	Thermom.				Wind.	Remarks.
	8 a.m.	Noon.	4 p.m.	8 p.m.		
Sat. 1	0	6	0	—2	Easterly.	Dark cloudy weather.
Sund. 2	0	—1	—2	—3	N.E.	Cloudy.
Mon. 3	0	—7	—6	—2	Variable.	Clear and cloudy.
Tues. 4	4	8	8	8	S.E.	Snowing and drift.
Wed. 5	2	4	1	0	S.E.	Cloudy and snow drift.
Thurs. 6	—3	—7	—5	—8	N.E.	Heavy snow drift.
Frid. 7	—6	—5	—4	—2	N.E.	Heavy snow drift.
Sat. 8	—2	—2	—2	—2	N.E.	Fine and clear.
Sund. 9	—2	—2	—4	—5	S.S.W.	Hazy and dull.
Mon. 10	10	—12	—10	—8	N.W.	Clear.
Tues. 11	—3	—5	—3	0.5	N.N.W.	Clear.
Wed. 12	10	—2	—10	—10	W.N.W.	Thick and hazy.
Thur. 13	—5	1	2	2	S.E.	Heavy snow drift and cloudy
Frid. 14	—7	—8	—6	—4	N.E.	Cloudy and snow drift.
Sat. 15	—4	—4	—5	+2	N.E.	Generally clear.
Sun. 16	—0	10	—10	4	S.E.	Hazy and cloudy.
Mon. 17	—6	—10	—10	0	F.N.E.	Generally clear.
Tues. 18	—2	—5	—7	—9	N.W.	Clear, fine weather.
Wed. 19	—8	—4	—4	0	N.W.	Fine, agreeable, and clear.
Thur. 20	—8	—8	—9	—7	Westerly.	Clear and cloudy.
Frid. 21	—5	—5	—5	—3	S.S.W.	Gloomy and dull.
Sat. 22	3	3	3	5	S.	Occasional snow showers.
Sun. 23	—10	—12	—13	—5	Variable.	Cloudy and overcast.
Mon. 24	0	3	4	6	S.E.	Snowing all day.
Tues. 25	—6	—12	—14	—8	Calm.	Fine and clear.
Wed. 26	—3	—4	—12	—12	W.S.W.	Snow and drift.
Thur. 27	—15	—15	—17	—19	Westerly.	Constant snow drift.
Frid. 28	—25	—28	—27	—23	W. & N.W.	Heavy snow drift.
Sat. 29	—29	—30	—31	—32	West.	Heavy snow drift.
Sun. 30	—36	—36	—38	—38	West.	Heavy snow drift.

METEOROLOGICAL JOURNAL FOR DECEMBER, 1851.

Date.	Thermom.				Wind.	Remarks.
	8 a.m.	Noon.	4 p m.	8 p m.		
Mon. 1	—34	—34	—30	—31	Westerly.	Snow drift and cloudy.
Tues. 2	—26	—26	—25	—25	Ditto.	Snow drift and cloudy.
Wed. 3	—15	—15	—20	—18	Ditto.	Clear.
Thurs. 4	—18	—8	—8	—8	Ditto.	Cloudy and lowering.
Frid. 5	—9	—12	—12	—15	Ditto.	Much snow falling.
Sat. 6	—13	—12	—11	—11	w. & n.w.	Quite overcast.
Sund. 7	—6	—9	—9	—7	n.w.	Fine and clear.
Mon. 8	—13	—11	—9	--6	n.w.	Clear and snow showers.
Tues. 9	—12	—12	—14	—18	s.e.	Snow drift and clear.
Wed. 10	—25	—25	—24	—21	e.s.e.	Heavy snow drift.
Thur. 11	—22	—22	—23	—24	n.	Ditto.
Frid. 12	—21	—16	—13	—16	n. & n.w.	Ditto.
Sat. 13	—11	—21	—22	—22	n.w.	Snow drift and clear.
Sund. 14	—10	—8	—10	—10	w.n.w.	Gloomy.
Mon. 15	—8	—6	—9	—13	Variable.	Cloudy.
Tues. 16	—23	—22	—22	—13	n.	Snow and drift.
Wed. 17	—19	—17	—16	—23	n.w.	Fine and clear star and moon-
Thur. 18	—11	—15	—17	—15	w.n.w.	Fine and clear. [light by day
Frid. 19	—15	—16	—20	—14	Variable.	Snow and drift.
Sat. 20	—9	—8	—8	—8	n.	Heavy snow drift.
Sund. 21	—10	—9	—5	—13	e.n.e.	Clear starlight.
Mon. 22	—15	—20	—19	—18	w.n.w.	Clear.
Tues. 23	—9	—11	—15	—18	w.n.w.	Clear and snow drift.
Wed. 24	—18	—20	—20	—20	w.	Generally clear.
Thur. 25	—15	—15	—20	—25	Calm.	Beautifully clear.
Frid. 26	—25	—23	—23	—23	Calm.	Overcast.
Sat. 27	20	—18	—17	—18	s.e.	Hazy and overcast.
Sund. 28	—23	—23	—28	—30	w.n.w.	Haze.
Mon. 29	—28	—25	—23	—22	s.e.	Dull, lowering weather.
Tues. 30	—12	—10	—9	—7	s.e.	Snow showers and drift.
Wed. 31	—6	—5	—5	—8	s.s.e.	Cloudy.

METEOROLOGICAL JOURNAL FOR JANUARY, 1852.

Date.	8 a.m.	Noon.	4 p.m.	8 p.m.	Wind.	Remarks.
		Thermom.				
Thur. 1	—6	—6	—6	—6	s.e.	Dark and gloomy.
Fri. 2	—4	—2	—4	—12	Easterly.	Dark and gloomy.
Sat. 3	—18	—20	—20	—20	West.	Fine and clear.
Sun. 4	—20	—20	—20	—20	West.	Fine and clear.
Mon. 5	—20	—20	—22	—25	West&calm	Overcast.
Tues. 6	—22	—2)	—22	—20	Easterly.	Gloomy and overcast.
Wed. 7	—15	—13	—12	—12	s.e.&calm.	Snow and cloudy.
Thur. 8	—15	—13	—12	—10	s.s.e.	Cloudy.
Fri. 9	—15	—17	—21	—23	Variable.	Cloudy and clear.
Sat. 10	—24	—23	—22	—22	n.w.	Clear above head & snow drift
Sun. 11	—10	—7	—1	—15	Variable.	Snow all day. [below.
Mon. 12	—22	—22	—24	—25	n.w. gale.	Snow and drift.
Tues. 13	—23	—22	—23	—21	n.w. gale.	Snow and drift.
Wed. 14	—25	—25	—27	—28	North.	Snow drift & clear above head.
Thur. 15	—30	—30	—29	—29	North.	Snow drift.
Fri. 16	—34	—34	—36	—33	n. & n.e.	Snowing and drifting.
Sat. 17	—34	—37	—35	—22	n. & n.w.	Snow drift and clear.
Sun. 18	—10	—10	—15	—18	Variable.	Cloudy and clear.
Mon. 19	—20	—23	—25	—30	n. & n.w.	Clear.
Tues. 20	—24	—12	—10	—20	n.w. gale.	Snow drift and clear.
Wed. 21	—32	—33	-31	—40	n.w. mod.	Clear.
Thur. 22	—44	—40	—35	—32	Westerly.	Clear.
Fri. 23	—30	—29	-30	—31	Variable.	Clear.
Sat. 24	—33	—25	—25	—25	Variable.	Clear and cloudy.
Sun. 25	—25	—27	—27	—25	n. gale.	Snow drift and sky clear.
Mon. 26	—21	—21	—16	—16	Variable.	Clear.
Tues. 27	—15	—17	—15	—15	n.w.	Overcast.
Wed. 28	—17	—22	—17	—15	n. gale.	Snow and drift.
Thur. 29	—10	—17	—20	—18	n. & n.w.	Snow and drift.
Fri. 30	—15	—18	—15	—13	Variable.	Cloudy.
Sat. 31	—10	—12	—12	—15	Variable.	Cloudy.

METEOROLOGICAL JOURNAL FOR FEBRUARY, 1852.

Date.	Thermom. 8 a.m.	Thermom. Noon.	Thermom. 4 p.m.	Thermom. 8 p.m.	Wind.	Remarks.
Sund. 1	—11	—9	—7	—6	E.S.E.	Cloudy.
Mon. 2	—30	Zero	Zero	+1	S.F.	Snowing throughout.
Tues. 3	+3	+2	+2	+2	East gale.	Snowing throughout.
Wed. 4	—1	+2	+1	—3	E strong gale	Snowing and drifting.
Thur. 5	—18	—21	—22	—27	Variable.	Cloudy and hazy.
Fri. 6	—30	—36	—37	—34	Variable.	Clear and cloudy.
Sat. 7	—33	—32	—29	—19	N.W.	Clear.
Sun. 8	—12	—9	—8	—6	N.E.	Cloudy and haze.
Mon. 9	—1	—1	—3	—6	N.N.E.	Cloudy and clear.
Tues. 10	—16	—18	—21	—19	Variable.	Cloudy and snow drift.
Wed. 11	—27	—29	—27	—23	N.E.	Clear and cloudy.
Thur. 12	—18	—20	—22	—23	N. & N.E.	Generally clear.
Fri. 13	—24	—27	—29	—27	w.n.w. gale	Snow drift.
Sat. 14	—23	—22	—23	—28	w.n.w. gale	Snow drift.
Sun. 15	—35	—32	—32	—32	N.W.	Fine and clear.
Mon. 16	—24	—26	—27	—33	Westerly.	Clear.
Tues. 17	—35	—32	—36	—39	Westerly.	Clear.
Wed. 18	—37	—34	—35	—35	Westerly.	Clear.
Thur. 19	—26	—19	—20	—22	N.W.	Clear.
Fri. 20	—20	—15	—22	—24	Variable.	Clear.
Sat. 21	—28	—28	—31	—31	N. & N.E.	Clear.
Sun. 22	—32	—26	—30	—32	Calm.	Clear.
Mon. 23	—32	—28	—28	—14	Variable.	Clear and cloudy.
Tues. 24	—12	—10	—12	—14	N. & N.E.	Frequent snow showers.
Wed. 25	—17	—17	—21	—18	Variable.	Clear.
Thur. 26	—26	—28	—28	—27	N.W.	Clear and cloudy.
Fri. 27	—26	—4	—4	Zero	Variable.	Gloomy and overcast.
Sat. 28	+4	+10	+10	+11	E. & E.N.E.	Cloudy and clear.
Sun. 29	+6	+10	+2	—5	Variable.	Clear weather.

METEOROLOGICAL JOURNAL FOR MARCH, 1852.

Date.	Thermom.				Winds.	Remarks.
	8 a.m.	Noon.	4 p.m.	8 p.m.		
Mon. 1	—9	— 7	—7	—7	N N.E. gale.	Snowing and drifting.
Tues. 2	—7	—3	—4	—4	N.N.E. gale.	Snowing and drifting.
Wed. 3	—14	—12	—12	—12	Variable.	Snowing and drifting.
Thur. 4	—14	—14	—14	—18	Variable.	Snowing and clear.
Fri. 5	—20	—15	—15	—19	Variable.	Clear.
Sat. 6	—26	—22	—23	—25	W.N.W. mod.	Cloudy and clear.
Sun. 7	—25	—5	—12	—19	W.N.W.	Cloudy.
Mon. 8	—25	—14	—19	—17	Calm.	Cloudy.
Tues. 9	—15	—8	—17	—33	Calm.	Cloudy.
Wed. 10	—38	Zero	—28	—37	Clear.	Fine and clear.
Thur. 11	—39	—19	—24	—30	Variable.	Cloudy and haze.
Fri. 12	—29	—22	—22	—28	Westerly.	Cloudy and haze.
Sat. 13	—28	—10	—20	—37	Westerly.	Cloudy.
Sun. 14	—30	—15	—29	—46	Variable.	Fine and clear.
Mon. 15	—39	—18	—26	—30	Variable.	Clear and snow drift.
Tues. 16	—33	—18	—28	—34	N. strong.	Clear and cloudy.
Wed. 17	—38	—20	—29	—39	N.W. mod.	Cloudy.
Thur. 18	—21	—12	—14	—14	E.N.E. gale	Snow drift.
Fri. 19	—21	—15	—15	—15	E.N.E. gale	Thick weather.
Sat. 20	—11	—5	—5	—5	E N.E. gale.	Same weather.
Sun 21	—6	—1	—15	—20	S.S.E.strong.	Snow and drift.
Mon. 22	—19	+12	+18	+20	E.by N. gale.	Heavy snow and drift.
Tues. 23	+22	+19	+17	+11	Variable.	Heavy wet snow.
Wed. 24	—5	+9	+4	—3	West.	Clear.
Thur. 25	Zero	+6	+5	+1	E.N.E strong	Cloudy and snow drift.
Fri. 26	+14	+10	+6	—15	N.E. strong.	Heavy snow.
Sat. 27	—18	+10	—4	—5	W.N.W.	Cloudy.
Sun. 28	—6	+7	—8	—10	Variable.	Cloudy.
Mon. 29	—21	—7	—24	—25	East.	Cloudy.
Tues. 30	—23	—10	—19	—24	N.W.	Clear.
Wed. 31	—15	—6	—9	—8	Variable.	Cloudy and hazy.

METEOROLOGICAL JOURNAL FOR
APRIL, 1852.

Date.	Thermom.				Wind.	Remarks.
	8 a m.	Noon.	4 p m.	8 p.m.		
Thur. 1	Zero	+6	+3	+1	n.w. mod.	Cloudy.
Fri. 2	Ze.o	+13	+2	+1	n.w. mod.	Cloudy.
Sat. 3	1	15	1	1	n.w.	Cloudy.
Sun. 4	—10	6	—4	—15	n.w. strong	Snow drift.
Mon. 5	—18	20	—12	—13	n.w. light.	Clear and cloudy.
Tues. 6	—5	13	—12	—12	Variable	Fine clear weather.
Wed. 7	—7	—3	—14	—1ᵣ	n.w. mod.	Cloudy and overcast.
Thur. 8	—7	—4	—9	—17	n.w. light.	Hazy.
Fri. 9	—10	12	—11	—17	n.w. mod.	Fine and clear.
Sat. 10	—10	23	—11	—15	Calm.	Fine, clear and pleasant.
Sun. 11	—3	7	1	Zero	s e. mod.	Cloudy.
Mon. 12	Zero	23	—2	—8	West.	Fine clear weather.
Tues. 13	Zero	29	—3	—9	Variable.	Clear.
Wed. 14	Zero	16	2	2	Westerly.	Thick and hazy.
Thur. 15	Zero	12	12	10	s.e. light.	Thick and close.
Fri. 16	19	29	20	12	s.e. light.	Cloudy.
Sat. 17	16	37	2	—7	Variable.	Beautiful and clear.
Sun. 18	16	44	12	11	n.	Overcast and threatening.
Mon. 19	16	18	14	11	n.w. mod.	Dark, cloudy, and hazy.
Tues. 20	14	21	12	11	n.w. mod.	Dull heavy weather.
Wed. 21	16	16	12	10	n.w. light.	Cloudy and clear.
Thur. 22	11	20	15	14	East.	Snowing throughout.
Fri. 23	16	22	16	15	s.e. mod.	Hazy and snow.
Sat. 24	15	40	18	15	s.e. light.	Fine and clear.
Sun. 25	18	46	20	17	Variable.	Fine and clear.
Mon. 26	20	41	13	2	n.w.	Heavy fall of snow.

LIST OF SUBSCRIBERS

TO THE LATE

BRANCH EXPEDITION TO REGENT INLET

IN 1851.

	£.	s.	d.
Admiral Sir Francis Beaufort, K.C.B.	20	0	0
Capt. W. A. B. Hamilton, R N.	20	0	0
John Barrow, Esq., Admiralty	15	0	0
The Rev. Dr. Scoresby	6	0	0
Lieut. Halkett, R.N.	10	0	0
Lieut. Dayman, R.N.	5	0	0
Henry Harvey, Esq., Brighton	5	0	0
Collected at Portsmouth	1	4	0
Lieut. Henderson, R.N., ditto	1	0	0
Lieut. Simpkinson, R.N., ditto	3	0	0
Charles Brægue, Esq.	2	0	0
Capt. Ward, R.N.	1	0	0
Sir William Wiseman, Bart., R.N., H.M.S. "Excellent"	1	0	0
Lieut. Burrows, R.N., ditto	0	10	0
Lieut. Tottenham, R.N., ditto	0	10	0
Capt. C. Dalrymple Hay, R.N.	1	1	0
Sir R. H. Inglis, Bart., M.P.	5	0	0
Miss Inglis	5	0	0

	£.	s.	d.
John Halkett, Esq. . . .	5	0	0
Hudson Gurney, Esq. (2nd donation) .	20	0	0
Miss Gurney . . .	10	0	0
Hon. Henry Elliot . . .	50	0	0
Lady Simpkinson . . .	10	0	0
Mrs. Majendie	10	0	0
Miss Guillemard . . .	1	0	0
Subscription at Orkney . . .	6	10	0
Rev. T. W. Franklyn . .	5	0	0
Sympathiser	10	0	0
Rev. R. W. Suckling . . .	1	0	0
Charles Dayman, Esq. . . .	2	2	0
Miss Dayman . . .	1	0	0
G. Ditman, Esq.	1	1	0
Richard Rogers, Esq. . .	5	0	0
— Reed, Esq.	10	0	0
Mrs. Rainsford . . .	1	0	0
A. K. Isbister, Esq. . . .	5	0	0
Mrs. Watson . . .	3	0	0
— Cresswell, Esq. . . .	2	2	0
Liverpool:—			
Thos. B. Horsfall, Esq. . .	10	0	0
W. J. Horsfall, Esq. . .	10	0	0
J. D., per ditto . . .	10	0	0
Miss Horsfall . . .	5	0	0
Mrs. C. H. Horsfall . . .	1	0	0
Miss Horsfall . . .	1	1	0
Robert Ranken, Esq. . . .	10	0	0
Henry Steele, Esq. . .	10	0	0

Liverpool — *continued.*   £.   s.   d.

J. Torr, Esq.	1	1	0
J. D. Anderson, Esq.	10	0	0
Roger Lynn Jones, Esq.	5	0	0
W. Rathbone, Esq.	5	0	0
Messrs. Headlam and Langton	5	0	0
Messrs. Hawson, Aikin, and Co.	5	0	0
John Marriott, Esq.	5	0	0
Netlam Ivry, Esq.	5	0	0
Rev. W. D.	1	0	0
X.Y.Z.	1	0	0
Vincent King, Esq.	1	0	0
G. B. Denton, Esq.	1	1	0
George Glen, Esq.	1	1	0
Thomas Carson, Esq.	1	0	0
Thomas Morris, Esq.	1	1	0
Samuel Martin, Esq.	1	1	0
Thos. James, Esq.	1	0	0
W. J. Tomkinson, Esq.	1	1	0
Wm. Jones, Esq.	1	1	0
Nicholas Duckworth, Esq.	1	0	0
Wm. Darming, Esq.	1	0	0
Small subscriptions through Capt. King, R.N.	0	7	6
W. B. P. by do.	0	14	0
Mrs. Osneer, collected by	1	17	6
J. Stuart, Esq. Aberdeen	1	0	0
Mrs. Penny, do.	3	0	0
Messrs. Golding and Hay, do.	0	10	0
Messrs. Bousville	2	2	0
Messrs. Duthie, Aberdeen	13	0	0

P

	£.	s.	d.
Mrs. Loft	5	0	0
Miss Cleland, Edinburgh, collected by	1	18	3
By Mr. W. Horsfall	5	0	0
M. Odillon Barrot, of France	2	2	0
E. H. Maltby, Esq.	3	3	0
Mrs. Henry de Vesconte	10	0	0
W. J. Le Feuvre, Esq.	10	0	0
Small subscriptions through Capt. King, R. N.	0	8	0
A. B. C. through Capt. King	1	0	0
Sundry subscriptions	2	5	0
Lieut. Halkett, R. N. (2nd donation)	5	0	0
Wm. Cappin, Esq. Londonderry, collected by	18	10	0

The first List of Subscribers is published in Snow's Voyage of the Prince Albert in 1859.

THE END.

G. NORMAN, PRINTER, MAIDEN LANE, COVENT GARDEN.

Printed by Printforce, United Kingdom